S0-AIR-335

The Language of St. Louis, Missouri

American University Studies

Series XIII

Linguistics

Vol. 4

PETER LANG
New York · Berne · Frankfurt am Main

Thomas E. Murray

The Language of St. Louis, Missouri

Variation in the Gateway City

PETER LANG
New York · Berne · Frankfurt am Main

Library of Congress Cataloging-in-Publication Data

Murray, Thomas E. (Thomas Edward)
The Language of St. Louis, Missouri.

(American University Studies. Series XIII, Linguistics ; vol. 4)
Bibliography: p.
1. English language–Dialects–Missouri–Saint Louis.
2. English language–Social aspects–Missouri–Saint Louis.
3. English language–Variation. 4. Americanisms–Missouri–Saint Louis–Dictionaries. I. Title. II. Title: Language of Saint Louis, Missouri. III. Series.
PE3101.M8M87 1986 427'.977866 86-15225
ISBN 0-8204-0324-5
ISSN 0740-4557

CIP-Kurztitelaufnahme der Deutschen Bibliothek

Murray, Thomas E.:
The Language of S[ain]t Louis, Missouri : Variation in the Gateway City / Thomas E. Murray. - New York ; Berne ; Frankfurt am Main : Lang, 1986.
(American University Studies : Ser. 13, Linguistics ; Vol. 4)
ISBN 0-8204-0324-5

NE: American University Studies / 13

Printed by Weihert-Druck GmbH, Darmstadt (West Germany)

ACKNOWLEDGEMENTS

I have incurred a number of debts in the preparation of this book, some of which I will never be able to repay. Most obviously, perhaps, I owe much to the hundreds of St. Louisans who served as informants, especially those who patiently and selflessly contributed hours of time to a project that they may never quite have understood. The many friends that I made and the many conversations that I took part in undoubtedly constitute the most enjoyable part of this entire project.

Thanks also go to Professor James W. Hartman, who was kind enough to wade through an early--and very sloppy--draft of my manuscript and to make suggestions for its improvement; and to Professor Raven I. McDavid, Jr., who, just before he died, read the final version of my manuscript and encouraged me to publish it.

At The Ohio State University, Murray Beja, the Chair of the English Department, bent a few rules that allowed me to meet a publisher's deadline, and the College of Humanities supported my research through a Publications Grant.

Finally, and most of all, I thank my wife, Carmin, whose hugs have provided me with everything I needed to get through all of this.

T. E. M.
Columbus, Ohio

CONTENTS

1. INTRODUCTION

In reviewing the numerous dialectological and sociolinguistic studies done in the United States, it becomes immediately apparent that one pocket of virtually untouched wealth is the city of St. Louis, Missouri. This lack of investigation is surprising, not only because St. Louis has a particularly colorful settlement history and has grown to be one of the largest cities in the country and one of the most important centers of commerce and transportation in the Midwest (and few such thriving metropolises have been ignored in the past twenty–five years of sociolinguistic research), but also because of the widespread disagreement regarding the dialectal character of its residents' speech. Whereas Flexner (1976: 119), for example, labels the St. Louis area speakers as using Southern Dialect, Malmstrom and Ashley (1963: 43) consider the city strictly South Midland; Shuy (1967: 47, map 6) positions St. Louis as occurring almost exactly on the boundary separating the North Midland and South Midland, though Laird (1970: 156–57) depicts it as a Northern island in the midst of a sea of Highland Southern; and the conclusions of Dakin (1971: 35; cf. also Lance 1974a: 9–10) suggest that the Gateway City exists in a transitional area in which both North Midland and South Midland forms co–exist, often in the same speaker.

Preliminary work for a Missouri Atlas––in which the language of St. Louis would certainly have received at least some attention––was begun more than a generation ago (Malmstrom and Ashley 1963: 17), but those data have never been edited or published. Faries (1967) studied Missouri's lexicon, but limited her selection of informants to only those who were elderly, uneducated, and living in sparsely populated rural areas; thus although seven of her respondents resided in St. Louis County, the data they produced have obvious limitations.[1] The eastern affiliations of Missouri speech in general were analyzed by Pace (1965), but while a few of his informants were residents of St. Louis, his methodology was severely lacking in rigor and his conclusions were sufficiently vague to preclude his work from being a serious contribution to delineating the language variation of any single area.[2] Lance (1974a, 1974b, 1975, 1977) and Lance and Faries (1985) have written on Missouri dialects in general, and while St. Louis does of course appear on the maps of isoglosses they draw, their primary concern is with establishing the dialect boundaries of the entire state rather than just the St. Louis area. Lance and Slemons (1976), using data collected from Lance's students, conclude that the Gateway City is currently in a period of transition, with elderly speakers clinging to South Midland forms and younger speakers introducing North Midland terms and pronunciations. Such conclusions are useful in attempting to delineate overall patterns of usage (see Chapter 6), but their scope is somewhat limited and, again, methodological rigor is lacking to some degree. Finally, various other scholars over the past century have investigated the more popular and presumably more colorful aspects of Missouri speech-- including its creole dialect (Carriere 1939), Mark Twain's conceptions of its social and geographic linguistic variation (Pederson 1967, Carkeet 1979), and, of course, the language of southern Missouri, especially the Ozarks (Weeks 1891; Crumb 1903; Carr and Taylor 1907; Taylor 1923; Randolph 1926, 1927a, 1927b, 1927c, 1928a, 1928b, 1929a, 1929b, 1931, 1933; Randolph and Ingleman 1928; Allison 1929; Randolph and Sankee 1930a, 1930b, 1930c; Randolph and Spradley 1933; Randolph and Clemens 1936; and Randolph and Wilson 1953)--but always at the expense of ignoring the speech of the Gateway City.

More recently, Johnson (1976) wrote a master's thesis on the language of St. Louis, and although his conclusions (which will receive attention in Chapter 6) seem to be the most extensive published to date, they are nevertheless limited by his extremely small sample of only eleven informants. Since 1983, I have written extensively on various aspects of St. Louis speech (Murray 1983a, 1983b, 1984a, 1984b, 1984c, 1985a, 1985b, 1985c, 1985d, 1985e, in press a), but most of these topics are rather esoteric and serve, at best, as discussions of only very limited significance if one is trying to understand the whole of linguistic variation in the Gateway City. It becomes clear, then, to paraphrase one of Underwood's assertions regarding the dialect of the Mesabi Iron Range of Minnesota (1981: 2), that a thorough investigation of the language of St. Louis is clearly warranted.

I began just such an investigation in June of 1982, and in this book would like to report the results of that study. Because one of the hallmarks of most published dialectological and sociolinguistic research--and especially of that done on a large scale--is that it is rich in empirical data,[3] my primary goal here is merely to provide a thorough descriptive account of my findings under the general rubrics of phonology (47 items), morphology and syntax (110 items), and lexicon (96 items).

But data in isolation have limited usefulness,[4] so I will also present analyses of those data that seek to shed light on the following questions: (1) Can significant patterns in the language of St. Louis be discovered when that language is viewed as a function of such independent variables as the age, gender, and socioeconomic class of its users? (2) How does the language of St. Louis compare to known dialectal patterns in the eastern United States, in Missouri, and in Illinois? (3) Why is the language of St. Louis as it is? (That is, are social class lines and geographic patterns of settlement solely responsible for the current linguistic state of affairs in the Gateway City, or are there other, perhaps equally important factors that bear on a St. Louisan's speech patterns?)

Answers to these questions will be offered in Chapter 6, following presentations of the phonology, morphology and syntax, and lexicon of St. Louis in Chapters 3, 4, and 5, respectively. Before moving directly to the data, however, some accounting must be made of the methods used in this study, and it is this topic to which I turn in Chapter 2.

2. METHODS

Carkeet (1979: 316) has written that "it is a characteristic flaw of published research in dialectology to dwell ponderously on methodological preliminaries," and he posits the reason for this as being "to disguise leanness in the body of [data]." Although I do not wish to be guilty of the same error, I nevertheless feel that a few pages devoted to the methods used in this study is both appropriate and necessary. At the very least, some remarks are certainly in order regarding precisely what was done and with whom, as well as how and why it was done that way, or the study would lose a certain amount of credence and replicability. It is these points, then, that will be considered in the two major sections of this chapter.

Procedures of the Study

The procedures used in this study can be divided into two distinct categories: those that parallel the traditional methods of dialectology as practiced, for example, by the fieldworkers of the various Linguistic Atlas projects, and those that fall squarely into the realm of sociolinguistics as practiced by a growing number of ethnographic participant–observers. Some may criticize this eclectic union, but the vast majority of researchers have come to realize that the goals and needs of their work are frequently met far more satisfactorily by combining the best aspects of two or more fundamentally different paradigms than they would have been through a strict allegiance to only one of them. In the following discussion, then, I will merely describe the major procedures I followed in the present study (cf. also Murray 1984e), and assume a thorough defense of them to be unnecessary.

Initially, the research reported here was intended to be strictly parallel and complementary to the several Linguistic Atlas projects: suitable and willing informants would be located, data would be collected through the use of questionnaires and personal interviews, and valid conclusions would be drawn concerning the language of St. Louis. Unfortunately, a major problem arose almost immediately. After securing my informants (about whom more will be said in the second section of this chapter) and beginning my interviews, it became apparent that although traditional techniques would suffice more than adequately for the collection of data on morphology, syntax, and lexicon, they were not at all suitable for the procurement of phonological data. Not only were my informants extremely uneasy when they became aware that I was observing their pronunciation, they quite obviously tried to effect certain changes in the formation of many of their vowels and consonants.[1] Even my attempts to lure them into a number of different stylistic shifts proved fruitless: neither the well-known "danger of death" question (cf. Labov 1972: 92–94) nor any other technique could diminish their phonological self-consciousness.

In truth, I must confess that such a reaction did not surprise me. Not only does the Hawthorne Effect come into play in such situations (i.e., a person's behavior changes just because of his or her perception of being a watched participant in some experiment; cf. Roethlisberger 1949, Murray 1982: 43, and Murray 1984e), but, being a native St. Louisan, I am especially aware that many Gateway City speakers are insecure about their pronunciation (about which more in Chapter 6). In any case, the unsuitability of my original methods for the collection of phonological data led me to experiment with new techniques, foremost among which was the frequent adoption of the role of ethnographic participant–observer. Whereas my preliminary interviews had been attempted in a very traditional way, with the tape recorder in full view of the informants and my identity as a person interested in language unconcealed, I now attempted to enter existing contexts (as opposed to "creating" new ones with the appearance of my tape recorder; cf. Murray 1982: 6–7) and collect data without revealing either my identity or my purpose.[2]

My preliminary interviews, in spite of being ultimate failures, were successful in that they provided me with a set of sounds about which many of my informants seemed to be especially wary of producing (and these sounds were augmented slightly by my own preconceived notions regarding salient variation in St. Louis phonology);[3] thus my task merely became one of (1) locating contexts of varying formality (cf. Murray 1982: 35–42, 140–48, Murray 1984a, and Murray 1984e) in which these sounds were produced frequently and by a wide range of people, (2) entering the contexts, collecting data, and then leaving without being detected, and (3) classifying each informant demographically and each speech sound stylistically. Contrary to my initial expectations and fears, the second of these tasks was by far the easiest. Armed with a pocket tape recorder, or, when background noise was prohibitive, a small notebook and pencil, I found I could move around quite easily without being detected. And on those few occasions when my recording was discovered, a bit of fast explaining usually soothed even the most perplexed or apprehensive of people.

Locating basic contexts also proved rather simple. I collected data in such diverse places as singles bars and funeral parlors (see Murray 1985b, Murray 1983a, and Murray 1984b), grocery stores and churches, laundromats and restaurants, gas stations and playgrounds, and, in short, anyplace where I could work relatively inconspicuously.[4] Varying the formality of each context and securing data from a wide variety of people, however, were considerably more problematic. The first of these was often accomplished in a manner similar to that followed by Labov (1972: 43–69) in his well–known department store survey: successive repeatings of the same sound with added emphasis each time were counted as fitting into different levels of speech formality. Elsewhere I had to rely on my own judgment for classifying language as "informal" (e.g., casual encounters), "midformal" (e.g., encounters in which one person is trying to perform a service for another person, as in restaurants and department stores), and "formal" (e.g., sermons and other public language). At no time, of course, was a context classified according to the language produced in it.

Even more problematic was the demographic classification of each informant. Although the male versus female distinction was usually quite straightforward ("usually" because St. Louis does seem to have an inordinately high population of androgynous beings, supplemented with the typically small subcultures of transvestites, bearded women, and so on), age and social class cannot always be determined so easily, and, moreover, the possibility constantly exists that an informant is not even a native St. Louisan. For the assignment of social class, I relied largely on the location of the context being investigated: patrons of those restaurants located in an upper–class section of St. Louis, for example, were counted as upper–class informants; shoppers of grocery stores in a middle–class part of the city were counted as middle–class informants; and users of laundromats in a lower–class neighborhood were labeled lower–class informants. (This procedure essentially parallels that followed by Labov in his department story survey, and even though I have criticized that technique elsewhere––see Murray 1982: 25, n. 10––I had to rely on it in the absence of any more sophisticated method.)

In checking my assessments of people's ages and determining that my informants were indeed native St. Louisans, I resorted to a simple but effective procedure: I asked approximately one out of every ten of them how old they were and what their status as residents of the city was. Though my queries received quite a number of raised eyebrows as initial responses, most people finally answered willingly and even sympathetically when they discovered that I was (1) a new federal (or state or city) employee assigned the tedious task of compiling demographic statistics for the Department of Consumer Affairs (or the state or city equivalent), and the security of my job rested on my ability to gather such data; (2) employed in a similar capacity for the owner or manager of the establishment that they were patronizing, and that the owner or manager needed the information to be able to serve customers more efficiently; or (3) a dear friend of someone who bore him or her an amazing resemblance, but who lived in another state and was a few years younger or older and on the brink of death. (Others wishing to apply these kinds of techniques to their own work should be advised that this last option is far more inefficient in obtaining results than the first two.) This method of random sampling assured me that my demographic labeling as to age was extremely accurate (above 90 percent), as was my luck in choosing informants who were lifelong St. Louisans (above 95 percent). All doubtful cases, of course, were discarded in the final analysis.

The Speech Community

I have already described the people who served as informants for the phonological part of this study, but here I would like to comment on the residents of St. Louis as a whole and also make some remarks concerning the informants I used for the sections on morphology, syntax, and lexicon.[5]

To begin, St. Louis--as also most other major cities in the United States--can only be described as a cosmopolitan blend of socioeconomic, geographic, and ethnic cultures. Beginning with the original French settlement of 1764, which was followed by a nearly 40-year rule of the area by the Spanish, the city expanded quickly into the Gateway to the West, especially after early 1804, when the transfer of the northern section of the Louisiana Purchase occurred there. Situated at the confluence of the Missouri, Mississippi, and Illinois Rivers, St. Louis attracted groups of merchants, craftsmen, farmers, and explorers--in short, people from all walks of life. Before about 1850 or 1860, most of these settlers, like most of the Missouri population in general, came from Kentucky, Tennessee, Virginia, the

Carolinas, and Maryland, or what is recognized linguistically as the South and South Midlands; however, post–Civil War migrants tended to have their roots in Illinois, Indiana, Ohio, Pennsylvania, and New York, or the North and North Midland speech areas. And after about 1900, the Deep South was well–represented in St. Louis by heavy migrations of (largely black) settlers from Alabama, Mississippi, and Georgia. Furthermore, additional thousands of settlers came directly from Europe: English, Scottish, and Spanish people all made their new homes in St. Louis, though not in numbers as large as did the French, Dutch, Italians, Czechs, Poles, and especially the Germans and Irish.[6]

Interestingly, though all these people of such diverse geographic, ethnic, and ideologic backgrounds seem to have co–existed in relative peace, there was not any extensive intermingling among them, at least ethnically. The Dutch and Czechs took up residence in South St. Louis, the Italians congregated in the Southwest, and the Irish, Poles, French, and Germans lived in the North. Some of my elderly informants recall this segregation of cultures as being so extensive that it was rare even as late as the early 1900s for children of different backgrounds to play together, and although some ethnic levelling has occurred in the twentieth century, despite any popular notions concerning American culture to the contrary, modern St. Louis is still no great melting pot. Indeed, vestiges of the original ethnic settlements in the city still remain: the Irish area only relative recently lost its nickname of Kerry Patch, the Pennsylvania Dutch Germans are still widely known as Scrubby Dutch (after their diligence in keeping clean the white stone steps of their front porches), the Czechs take great pride in their athletic organization Socol, and the Italians live on The Hill and have made Hill Day a widely–attended annual fall celebration.

It becomes clear, then, that the linguist who wishes to study "the" language of St. Louis faces the problem of selecting informants that will not bias the final results of the study. Rather than choosing equal numbers of each ethnic sub–population of the city, I elected to avoid "pure" informants as much as possible. None of the ethnographic collecting of data reported above was done in strongly ethnic sections of the city, just as none of my other informants came from any but an ethnically mixed background. Furthermore, because one of the requirements to be met by all non–phonological informants was that both they and their parents had to have lived in St. Louis all of their lives, all of my data come from the mouths of white speakers. It is true that inner St. Louis is now populated almost exclusively by blacks, but the vast majority were born in other parts of the country and then migrated to the Gateway City; thus I could not, strictly speaking, label their speech "the language of St. Louis."

All of my informants for the morphology, syntax, and lexicon isections of this study, then, were ethnically–mixed caucasians who have lived, along with their parents, in St. Louis all their lives. Moreover, none had traveled or studied elsewhere for a period of time sufficient to have affected his or her speech. The only remaining problem was to decide how many to place in which demographic cells. The independent variables I chose to investigate are social class (upper, middle, lower), gender, and age (under 20, 20–40, 40–60, and 60–80). Social class was determined through the use of conventional criteria such as occupation, education, salary, and place of residence; and the only stipulation on the variable of age was that the "under 20" informants all be post–pubescent so that their language could be regarded as "fixed." Regarding the quantity of people needed to fill each demographic cell, Wolfram and Shuy (1974: 39–40) have recommended that a minimum of five be used to preclude any chance of statistical bias. In the present study, I have chosen to double that figure; thus a total of 240 informants occur in 24 demographic cells (10 of each gender in each age group in each socioeconomic class; see Fig. 1). Finally, none of the 240 informants is immediately related to any of the others.[7]

upper class								middle class								lower class							
male				female				male				female				male				female			
< 20	20- 40	40- 60	60- 80	< 20	20- 40	40- 60	60- 80	< 20	20- 40	40- 60	60- 80	< 20	20- 40	40- 60	60- 80	< 20	20- 40	40- 60	60- 80	< 20	20- 40	40- 60	60- 80

Fig. 1: Demographic Distribution of Informants

3. PHONOLOGY

The paradigmatic shift from structural to generative phonology over the past generation has caused numerous problems for those linguists who recognize the value both of charting surface phonetic variants (to gain insight into dialectal patterns) and of determining underlying phonemic structures and their accompanying generative rules (to gain insight into the psychological and social reality of phonological forms and the putative corellary psychological and social reality of their users). Typically, one method of analysis and interpretation is chosen to the exclusion of the other, and although the two paradigms have thus co–existed since the early 1960s––each being used frequently and enthusiastically by a number of scholars––Underwood's remark concerning the "superior power of generative phonology over structural phonemics" is instructive in predicting the future use of structuralism alone: "the study of the sound system of any dialect is incomplete without generative phonology" (1981: 51).

In the present study, admittedly, the phonological analysis is primarily structural in nature. Although I will attempt to give as thorough an account of phonetic variation in the language of St. Louis as possible, and even offer a tentative, somewhat primitive constraint for the phonetic realization of pre–retroflex /o/ as a low back vowel, my goals are primarily descriptive rather than explanatory; thus underlying phonemes will not usually be posited and no generative rules will be written. These matters, though of course important, can be addressed more easily and with greater relevance in a study that is primarily theoretical rather than descriptive.

The presentation of data in this chapter is organized parallel to the manner in which the initial analyses were completed, and is structured as a set of answers to the following three questions: (1) Is the phoneme being analyzed a consonant or a vowel? (2) Is the phonetic occurrance or realization of that phoneme categorical or variable? (3) If the phoneme is variable, does it occur in free variation or is its variation conditioned?[1]

Consonants

Categorical

1. postvocalic /r/

2. initial phoneme of ***whip***, ***wheel***, ***wheelbarrow***, etc.

The deletion of postvocalic /r/ that is so common in New England and the South never occurs in the speech of St. Louisans, the only exception being the /r/ in ***quarter***, which will be discussed separately below. And although the initial phoneme of ***whip***, ***wheel***, and other such ***wh***– words is very infrequently recognized phonetically as Northern [hw], Southern and Midlands [w] can, for all practical purposes, be considered a categorical usage. See Table 1.

variable: free variation

3. initial phoneme of ***humor***

4. final phoneme of ***garage***

5. <th> of ***with*** and ***without***

The phonetic realization of each of each of these phonemes in the language of St. Louis is unpredictable: the initial phoneme of ***humor*** occurs as both Midlands [j] and Northern/Southern [hj], though [j] typically enjoys a slight preference, as shown in Table 2; the final phoneme of ***garage*** is realized as both the voiced affricate and the voiced palatal fricative, though the affricate is always favored a bit more often than the fricative; and the <th> in ***with*** and ***without***, though usually pronounced as the Northern voiced interdental fricative, occurs almost as often phonetically as the voiceless Midlands counterpart.

TABLE 1
CONSONANTS SHOWING CATEGORICALITY

sound in question	socioeconomic class of informants	contextual formality					
		informal		midformal		formal	
		%	n	%	n	%	n
postvocalic /r/ (% retained)	upper	100	105	100	120	100	89
	middle	100	119	100	151	100	111
	lower	100	113	100	126	100	93
initial [w]/[hw] (% [w])	upper	100	108	99	122	99	74
	middle	100	143	100	176	99	127
	lower	100	132	100	138	100	115

variable: conditioned variation

TABLE 2
CONSONANTS SHOWING FREE VARIATION

sound in question	socioeconomic class of informants	informal %	informal n	midformal %	midformal n	formal %	formal n
initial sound of *humor* (% [j])	upper	52	118	43	123	56	112
	middle	59	126	52	142	53	120
	lower	57	189	51	109	48	83
final sound of *garage* (% affricate)	upper	58	115	61	123	54	132
	middle	54	98	56	111	56	108
	lower	59	113	51	99	56	116
<th> sound of *with(out)* (% voiced)	upper	61	112	56	109	47	89
	middle	56	104	54	97	55	113
	lower	52	118	47	91	51	100

6. intrusive [r]

St. Louisans, like other speakers in the Midlands dialect area, are widely known and easily recognized for their ability to insert [r] into *wash*–containing composites such as *washer* and *Washington*. Indeed, one can become aware of the pervasiveness of this intrusive [r] in the Gateway City without even hearing it: several laundromats in the area sport "out of order" signs that read "warsher broke" or "warsher don't work," and I can recall seeing on one occasion "warsher don't work" scratched out and replaced with "warsher ***doesn't*** work" (emphasis in original) by a would–be grammarian who either had a highly developed linguistic sense of humor or was so used to pronouncing the intrusive [r] that he failed to correct it. (All of this leads one to muse whether ***warsh*** will ever become as accepted as ***sherbert***, which now appears on several commercial brands of a food that looks and tastes remarkably like "sherbet.") In any case, Table 3 shows that all St. Louisans (even those corresponding to the Group III "cultured, well–educated" speakers of the Atlas projects) allow [r] to intrude into their speech; it is not the case, as some linguists have maintained (see, e.g., McDavid 1972: 33), that only "old–fashioned, rustic, poorly–educated speakers" and "younger, more modern, and better–educated speakers" (i.e., Atlas groups I and II, respectively) exhibit the trait. Furthermore, [r] seems to intrude less often in the speech of informants from all social classes as they perceive themselves as being in increasingly formal contexts.

7. [s]/[z] alternants in ***grease***, ***greasy***, ***sink***, and ***isolate*** (***–ed***, ***–s***, ***–ing***, ***–tion***)

I expanded the typical analysis of [s]/[z] in ***grease*** and ***greasy*** to include (kitchen) ***sink*** and ***isolate*** (in all of its forms) to afford myself the opportunity to study both initial and final variation as well as variation occurring before and after primary stress. A summary of my findings appears in Table 4, which shows clearly that Northern and North Midlands [s] is the pronunciation St. Louisans perceive as the prestige standard. This observation is especially true, it seems, among speakers under the age of 60 and when ***s*** occurs initially; older speakers, conversely, are more willing to use Southern and South Midlands [z] in all positions.

8. initial phoneme of ***yeast***

Yeast can be pronounced in St. Louis as either [jist] or [ist], the only difference being the occurrance or non–occurrance of the initial palatal /j/. As shown in Table 5, the [j]–less pronunciation increases markedly in all speakers over 60, and although contextual informality correlates with the increased phonetic realization of /j/ as the empty set, it is interesting that no elderly, lower–class informant pronounced the initial sound of the word as [j].

TABLE 3
CONDITIONED VARIATION OF INTRUSIVE [r]

sound in question	socioeconomic class of informants	informal		midformal		formal	
		%	n	%	n	%	n
intrusive [r] (% pronounced)	upper	83	1446	68	1185	39	679
	middle	92	1657	76	1369	52	937
	lower	99	1766	82	1463	68	1213

9. *l* of ***palm***

The *l* in ***palm*** can be recognized phonetically by St. Louisans as either [l] or as the empty set. Table 6 indicates that only upper–class speakers typically choose [l], although members of the middle class pronounce the *l* in formal contexts slightly more often that not. *l* appears not to occur at all in the speech of the lower class.

10. *r* of *quarter*

TABLE 4
CONDITIONED VARIATION OF [s]/[z]

sound in question	socioeconomic class of informants	placement of *s* in word	age of informants	contextual formality					
				informal		midformal		formal	
				%	n	%	n	%	n
[s]/[z] (% [z])	upper	initial	under 60	0	0	0	0	0	0
			over 60	9	34	2	8	0	0
		medial	under 60	0	0	0	0	0	0
			over 60	31	216	19	132	8	56
	middle	initial	under 60	23	166	9	65	0	0
			over 60	38	165	24	104	7	30
		medial	under 60	47	571	39	473	23	279
			over 60	62	526	51	432	34	288
	lower	initial	under 60	29	198	22	150	14	96
			over 60	47	193	33	135	24	98
		medial	under 60	69	698	61	617	48	485
			over 60	82	640	73	570	57	445

TABLE 5
CONDITIONED VARIATION OF [j] IN *yeast*

sound in question	socioeconomic class of informants	age of informants	contextual formality					
			informal		midformal		formal	
			%	n	%	n	%	n
[j]/empty set (% [j])	upper	under 40	100	298	100	314	100	301
		40-60	93	312	100	323	100	284
		over 60	22	71	33	113	62	162
	middle	under 40	100	300	100	309	100	302
		40-60	74	233	83	269	96	297
		over 60	2	7	10	32	31	111
	lower	under 40	88	301	93	315	100	362
		40-60	56	148	69	219	89	310
		over 60	0	0	0	0	0	0

I mentioned earlier (see # 1) that St. Louisans never delete post–vocalic *r*, the only exception to that rule being in their pronunciation of ***quarter***. As Table 7 makes clear, the *r* of ***quarter*** is both a social and a stylistic marker in the language of St. Louis: its deletion varies both according to the socioeconomic class of the speaker and to the formality of the context in which the speaker is speaking. All social classes delete the sound, though that deletion becomes more frequent as one descends the socioeconomic scale; and it is deleted in all contexts, though, again, more frequently as contextual formality decreases.

TABLE 6
CONDITIONED VARIATION OF [l] IN palm

sound in question	socioeconomic class of informants	contextual formality					
		informal		midformal		formal	
		%	n	%	n	%	n
[l]/empty set (% [l])	upper	66	214	79	260	90	319
	middle	10	28	29	81	52	162
	lower	0	0	0	0	0	0

11. pronunciation of ***mrs.***

The pronunciation of ***mrs.*** is one of the most interesting phonological phenomena in the language of St. Louis: not only is there variation according to the socioeconomic class of the speaker and the formality of the context, but as Table 8 shows, the age and gender of the speaker also play significant roles in determining whether Northern and North Midlands [mIsIz] or Southern and South Midlands

[mIz] is used. I should also point out, perhaps, that the problem of identifying [mIsIz] and [mIz] speakers has been further exacerbated by the introduction of ***ms.*** as an alternative for ***mrs.*** and ***miss.*** Many former [mIsIz] speakers now say [mIz] not because of a phonological reduction of ***mrs.***, but because they have adopted ***ms.*** in its place; and many former [mIz] speakers, who were quite content to reduce ***mrs.*** to a single syllable, now make an extra effort to say [mIsIz] because they do not want to be identified as users of ***ms.*** It thus becomes impossible to distinguish those speakers whose pronunciation is determined solely by phonological processes from those whose pronunciation is tempered by ideological beliefs. That caveat aside, however, Table 8 indicates that the frequency of [mIsIz] rises in direct proportion to the social class of the speaker and the formality of the context in which it occurs, and, further, that all males under the age of 60 use [mIsIz] more often than do their female counterparts. Finally, [mIsIz] also occurs most often among males between 40 and 60 and among females over 60.

Vowels

Categorical

12. vowel in ***bath***, ***glass***, ***aunt***, and all other ***a + fricative*** and ***a + nasal*** words except ***pajamas***, ***pecan***, and ***plaza*** (cf. # 29 below)

13. vowel in ***pen***, ***penny***

14. vowel in ***fog***, ***log***, ***on***

15. stressed vowel in ***foreign***, ***orange***

16. stressed vowel in ***water***

17. stressed vowel in ***Mary***, ***marry***, ***merry***

18. stressed vowel in ***either***, ***neither***

19. unstressed vowel in ***stomach***

20. diphthong in ***bite***, ***kite***, etc.

21. diphthong in ***house***, ***about***, etc.

Table 9 shows clearly that St. Louisans assign relatively categorical usage status to each of the ten above–named vowels and diphthongs: pre–fricative ***a*** always occurs as the low–front rather than the low–central vowel except in ***pajamas***, ***pecan***, and ***plaza***; the vowels in ***pen*** and ***penny*** are uniformly of the Northern/Midlands mid–front lax rather than the Southern high–front lax variety;[2] the vowels in ***fog***, ***log***, and ***on*** are uniformly of the Southern/Midlands low–back rather than the Northern low–central or any other variety; the low–back vowel rather than the low–central or mid–back vowel also occurs as the stressed vowel in ***foreign*** and ***orange***; St. Louisans use the low back vowel rather than the low central vowel as the stressed vowel in ***water***; ***Mary***, ***marry***, and ***merry*** are all homonyms pronounced with the Midlands mid–front lax vowel in the stressed position; the stressed vowel of ***either*** and ***neither*** occurs as [i] rather than any diphthong; St. Louisans use the Midlands high–front lax vowel rather than the Northern/Southern mid–central vowel in the unstressed syllable of ***stomach***; and the diphthongs in ***bite*** and ***house*** are always of the Northern and North Midlands variety––that is, they begin with a low–central element and move either to a high– front lax or a high–back lax element––rather than any other. Considering both the diverse settlement history of St. Louis and the highly variable nature of many of the other phonemes reported in this chapter, the categoricality of these sounds is little short of amazing. That such phonological leveling has occurred is perhaps best understood at least in part as a reflex of the corresponding geographic and ethnic leveling noted in Chapter 2.

Free Variation

22. vowel in ***route***

23. vowel in *roof*

24. vowel in *hearth*

25. stressed vowel in *depot*

26. stressed vowel in *patronize*

27. stressed vowel in *because*

TABLE 7
CONDITIONED VARIATION OF r IN quarter

sound in question	socioeconomic class of informants	contextual formality: informal %	n	midformal %	n	formal %	n
	upper	51	167	42	133	34	117
r in quarter	middle	84	267	62	177	53	162
	lower	100	344	95	341	93	298

The data in Table 10 indicate that although one of the phonetic variants of each of the vowel phonemes listed above is often favored over the other possibilities in the speech of St. Louisans, it is impossible to predict with any accuracy which alternant will occur on any given occasion. Thus [u] occurs slightly more often than the low–central to high–back lax diphthong in *route*, but that usage is not patterned; St. Louisans largely use the Southern [ruf] rather than the Northern counterpart with the high–back lax vowel, but not predictably so; *hearth* can occur with the Midlands low–back vowel or the Northern/Southern mid–central vowel, and both have equal chances of occurring in all the same contexts; the high–front tense [i] rather than its mid–front lax counterpart is the preferred variant of the stressed vowel in ***depot***, but the two usages are in no way complementary; the mid–front tense and the low–front vowels both occur unpredictably in ***patronize***; and the stressed vowel in ***because*** is almost evenly divided between the Northern mid–central vowel and the Southern/Midlands low–back vowel, with all speakers as likely to use one variant as the other.

variable: ***conditioned variation***

28. pre–*r* /o/

St. Louisans often homophonize the pre–*r* contrast in pairs of words such as ***born/barn***, ***for/far***, ***former/farmer***, ***forty/farty***, ***lord/lard***, and so on to the Northern/North Midlands low–back vowel. Furthermore, they also often replace pre–r /o/ with its low–back variant even in words that have no such counterpart in Standard English––as in, for example, ***fork***, ***corpse***, ***scorpion***, ***corporation***, and ***sordid***. But this phenomenon is by no means random. As Table 11 shows, the low back vowel occurs more frequently as contextual formality and the social class of the speaker decrease. More important, perhaps, linguistic environment also plays a major role in determining the occurrance of the low–back vowel: it never occurs in my data when it is followed by final, silent *e* (e.g., ***bore***, ***core***, ***fore***, ***adore***, ***pore***, ***sore***, ***lore***, ***tore***, ***yore***, ***ore***, etc.), *t* in the same stressed syllable (***abort***, ***fort***, ***port***, ***sort***, ***retort***, ***portable***, ***wort***, ***torte***, etc.), or silent ***ps*** (e.g., ***corps***). I offer these, then, as tentative linguistic constraints for the occurrance of the low–back vowel before *r* in words spelled <. . . or . . .>, though of course a larger data base and further analysis are necessary to confirm and refine them.

29. vowel in ***pajamas***, ***pecan***, ***plaza***

I have already noted that pre–fricative and pre–nasal *a* is categorically recognized as the low–front vowel in the language of St. Louis (see # 12 above), but the conditioned occurrance of the low–central vowel [a] in ***pajamas***, ***pecan***, and ***plaza*** is

TABLE 8
CONDITIONED VARIATION IN THE PRONUNCIATION OF Mrs.

sound in question	socioeconomic class of informants	gender of informants	age of informants	contextual formality: informal %	informal n	midformal %	midformal n	formal %	formal n
			under 40	53	161	62	183	76	229
		male	40-60	72	274	81	280	94	298
			over 60	67	202	74	244	86	279
	upper		under 40	38	123	46	139	62	177
		female	40-60	48	149	61	176	74	213
			over 60	72	251	89	291	98	314
			under 40	44	137	52	153	64	188
		male	40-60	63	180	70	214	85	271
[mIsIz]/ [mIz] (% [mIsIz])	middle		over 60	51	153	60	174	72	206
			under 40	24	78	33	99	49	161

TABLE 8
CONDITIONED VARIATION IN THE PRONUNCIATION OF Mrs. (cont.)

sound in question	socioeconomic class of informants	gender of informants	age of informants	contextual formality: informal %	informal n	midformal %	midformal n	formal %	formal n
		female	40-60	41	131	49	142	64	182
			over 60	59	180	68	207	78	240
			under 40	21	75	29	94	37	120
		male	40-60	40	131	52	160	61	177
			over 60	32	111	41	130	51	156
	lower		under 40	8	29	19	69	33	112
		female	40-60	19	74	38	128	59	170
			over 60	38	127	52	161	66	192

an exception to that general rule. In these three words alone do the increased social class of the speaker, the increased formality of the context, and, to a lesser extent, the decreased age of the speaker combine to shift the low–front vowel back to its low–central counterpart. The relevant data can be found in Table 12.

30. vowel in *egg(s)*

Older St. Louisans, especially, as well as those non–upper–class members and those speaking in informal contexts, tend to tense the standard mid–front lax vowel in *egg(s)* to [e]. Table 13 indicates that the sound change from tense to lax has been in progress many years, and in fact now seems to be almost complete: [e] occurs among younger speakers only insignificantly.

31. vowel in ***due***, ***news***, stressed vowel in ***Tuesday***, ***coupon***, etc.

The two standard variants of the vowel in ***due***, ***news***, and the stressed vowel in ***Tuesday***, and ***coupon*** are Northern/North Midlands [u] and Southern/South Midlands [ju], and as the data in Table 14 reflect, St. Louisans overwhelmingly prefer [u]. (Because the data for ***coupon*** differ somewhat from those for the other other words, it has been given separate treatment in the Table.) Indeed, lower–class speakers use [u] almost exclusively, and middle–class speakers use [ju] only about one–fourth to one–fifth of the time. Only upper–class speakers use [ju] frequently, and even they revert to [u] in the most informal contexts.

32. vowel in ***catch***

The pronunciation of ***catch*** in St. Louis seems not to be affected by the social class of the speaker or the formality of the context in which it is spoken; rather, the salient variable is the age of the speaker. As Table 15 shows, St. Louisans over the age of 30 uniformly use the general mid–front lax vowel, whereas those under 30 sometimes use the low–front vowel.

33. vowel in ***creek***

All St. Louisans under the age of 30 are Northern/Southern/South Midlands [krik]–speakers, as are those over 30 who are members of the upper class. Other St. Louisans say the Northern/North Midlands variety of the word, with the high–front lax vowel, infrequently, and although there is no correlation with style of speech, lower–class speakers consistently use the Northern/North Midlands form of the word more often than do middle–class speakers. Table 16 contains all of the relevant data.

34. stressed vowel in ***bury***

Both the mid–central and the mid front lax vowel occur as the stressed vowel of ***bury*** in the language of St. Louis, and as Table 17 indicates, there is a correlation between usage and both style of speech and social class of speaker. The variety with the mid–front lax vowel is the favored pronunciation among all speakers in all situations except for members of the upper class who find themselves in very formal contexts.

35. stressed vowel in ***sausage***

Some St. Louisans pronounce ***sausage*** with the Southern low–central vowel in the stressed syllable; others pronounce it with the Northern low–back vowel in the stressed syllable. As reflected by the data in Table 17, the latter of these two variations is the favored pronunciation, although speakers over the age of 60 and especially those who are also members of the lower class prefer the former.

TABLE 9
VOWELS SHOWING CATEGORICALITY

Sound in question	socioeconomic class of informants	contextual formality					
		informal		midformal		formal	
		%	n	%	n	%	n
vowel in bath, etc. (% low-front)	upper	99	319	98	321	96	309
	middle	100	342	100	302	97	298
	lower	100	314	100	319	100	301
vowel in pen, penny (% mid-front lax)	upper	100	323	100	314	100	317
	middle	99	307	100	332	100	311
	lower	96	302	98	313	99	318
vowel in fog, log, on (% low-back	upper	100	333	100	299	100	309
	middle	99	289	100	280	100	315
	lower	100	297	100	302	100	320

TABLE 9
VOWELS SHOWING CATEGORICALITY (cont.)

Sound in question	socioeconomic class of informants	contextual formality					
		informal		midformal		formal	
		%	n	%	n	%	n
stressed vowel in foreign, orange (% low-back)	upper	97	314	95	283	95	291
	middle	100	311	100	323	98	288
	lower	100	322	100	331	100	293
stressed vowel in water (% low-back)	upper	100	304	100	314	100	287
	middle	99	289	100	280	100	315
	lower	100	297	100	302	100	320
stressed vowel in Mary, marry, merry (% mid-front lax)	upper	100	286	100	314	100	336
	middle	100	299	100	289	100	321
	lower	100	300	100	261	100	284

TABLE 9
VOWELS SHOWING CATEGORICALITY (cont.)

Sound in question	socioeconomic class of informants	contextual formality: informal %	informal n	midformal %	midformal n	formal %	formal n
stressed vowel in either, neither (% [i])	upper	100	281	98	266	96	300
	middle	100	306	100	271	100	331
	lower	100	314	100	274	100	309
unstressed vowel in stomach (% [I])	upper	100	327	100	285	100	319
	middle	100	311	100	341	100	280
	lower	98	322	100	338	100	296
diphthong in bite, etc. (% low-central to high-front)	upper	100	258	100	289	100	289
	middle	100	263	100	296	100	308
	lower	100	281	100	304	100	276

TABLE 9
VOWELS SHOWING CATEGORICALITY (cont.)

Sound in question	socioeconomic class of informants	contextual formality					
		informal		midformal		formal	
		%	n	%	n	%	n
diphthong in house, etc. (% low-central to high-back)	upper	100	292	100	313	100	316
	middle	100	259	100	297	100	322
	lower	100	277	100	296	100	315

TABLE 10
VOWELS SHOWING FREE VARIATION

sound in question	socioeconomic class of informants	contextual formality informal %	n	midformal %	n	formal %	n
vowel in route (% [u])	upper	54	161	60	184	58	191
	middle	54	158	56	170	57	183
	lower	48	149	52	151	51	162
vowel in roof (% [u])	upper	69	213	71	222	70	220
	middle	72	215	75	214	74	231
	lower	67	189	72	199	69	219
vowel in hearth (% low back)	upper	62	191	58	172	60	175
	middle	65	207	71	190	69	199
	lower	64	204	66	201	67	184
stressed vowel in depot (% [i])	upper	75	233	68	211	70	206
	middle	70	214	73	220	71	198
	lower	72	200	74	218	66	201

TABLE 10
VOWELS SHOWING FREE VARIATION (cont.)

sound in question	socioeconomic class of informants	informal %	informal n	midformal %	midformal n	formal %	formal n
stressed vowel in patronize (% [e])	upper	67	198	71	223	64	189
	middle	70	202	69	187	73	216
	lower	64	186	68	177	71	199
stressed vowel in because (% mid central)	upper	56	163	53	162	54	153
	middle	52	159	50	151	51	156
	lower	48	154	49	144	52	147

36. final vowel in *sundae*

Most St. Louisans are well aware of the joke concerning the pronunciation of ***sundae***: the entire United States is said to pronounce the word as containing the mid–front tense or high–front tense vowel in final position, with only the aboriginal natives of St. Louis pronouncing the word with a mid–central vowel in final position. I cannot speak to the truth of the first part of the joke, but my research provides considerable support for the second (that is, not that the natives of St. Louis are aboriginal, but that they do indeed use a mid–central vowel in the final position of ***sundae*** very frequently). Table 19 shows clearly that St. Louisans of all ages and socioeconomic levels prefer the mid–central vowel to either the mid–front

TABLE 11
CONDITIONED VARIATION OF PRE-r /o/

sound in question	socioeconomic class of informants	contextual formality: informal %	n	midformal %	n	formal %	n
pre-r /o/ (% low back)	upper	34	278	22	180	6	49
	middle	71	733	35	464	29	299
	lower	96	910	77	730	42	398
with constraints	upper	0	68	0	59	0	72
	middle	0	96	0	87	0	44
	lower	0	129	0	131	0	77

tense or high-front tense vowel in all styles of speech; the mid-front tense vowel occurs occasionally in the most formal styles of the upper classes, and the high-front tense vowel appears sporadically throughout St. Louis speech.[3]

37. final vowel in *Missouri*

There is a slight tendency for St. Louisans to have their pronunciation of *Missouri* tempered by linguistic environment--if the word is followed by a consonant (e.g., "Missour*i* *can*"), the final vowel occurs as mid-central more often than high-front tense, which is the frequent pronunciation when the word is followed by a vowel (e.g., "Missour*i* *and*")--but the vast majority of speakers use the high-front tense

TABLE 12

CONDITIONED VARIATION OF THE PRE–FRICATIVE/PRE–NASAL a IN *pecan*, *plaza*, and *pajamas*

sound in question	socioeconomic class of informants	age of informants	contextual formality: informal %	informal n	midformal %	midformal n	formal %	formal n
pre-nasal *a* (% [a])	upper	under 30	89	269	96	294	100	303
		30-60	62	191	92	256	98	314
		over 60	56	167	63	185	77	231
	middle	under 30	61	180	86	244	99	296
		30-60	46	132	75	227	89	263
		over 60	41	127	73	219	81	252
	lower	under 30	0	0	4	11	16	46
		30-60	0	0	0	0	9	29
		over 60	0	0	0	0	6	21

TABLE 13
CONDITIONED VARIATION OF e IN egg(s)

sound in question	socioeconomic class of informants	age of in-formants	contextual formality: informal %	informal n	midformal %	midformal n	formal %	formal n
vowel in egg(s) (% [e])	upper	under 60	0	0	0	0	0	0
		over 60	41	333	22	179	7	57
	middle	under 60	5	37	0	0	0	0
		over 60	65	513	49	356	37	292
	lower	under 60	9	64	1	7	0	0
		over 60	89	612	78	537	71	489

TABLE 14
CONDITIONED VARIATION OF [u]/[ju]

sound in question	socioeconomic class of informants	contextual formality: informal %	n	midformal %	n	formal %	n
vowel in due, news, etc. (% [u])	upper	77	236	55	161	42	138
	middle	97	294	90	269	81	242
	lower	100	314	100	351	100	301
coupon	upper	65	198	49	152	34	101
	middle	74	228	62	169	56	160
	lower	81	238	74	227	71	212

vowel in all styles of speech. To be sure, it is possible to hear rural schwa, in unguarded moments, even in the most formal of contexts--as, for example, during a televised newscast--but urban [i] is the pronunciation preferred in the Gateway City (cf. those sections of Table 20 depicting the phonetics of *Missouri* when it occurs sentence-finally).

38. final vowel in *tomato, potato*

Most members of the upper class recognize the final vowel of *potato* and *tomato* as Northern [o], as do members of the middle class speaking in all but the most informal of contexts. Elsewhere, Southern/Midlands centralized schwa is the favored pronunciation, as it is in all contexts for members of the lower class. As Table 21

TABLE 15
CONDITIONED VARIATION OF THE a IN catch

sound in question	socioeconomic class of informants	age of informants	contextual formality: informal %	informal n	midformal %	midformal n	formal %	formal n
vowel in catch (% mid-front lax)	upper	under 30	68	203	61	182	70	219
		over 30	100	277	100	281	100	278
	middle	under 30	63	195	64	191	59	175
		over 30	100	300	100	293	100	309
	lower	under 30	100	298	100	304	100	320
		over 30	100	287	100	311	100	292

TABLE 16
CONDITIONED VARIATION OF THE ee IN Creek

sound in question	socioeconomic class of informants	age of informants	contextual formality: informal %	informal n	midformal %	midformal n	formal %	formal n
vowel in creek (% [i])	upper	under 30	100	319	100	314	100	306
		over 30	100	288	100	311	100	282
	middle	under 30	100	302	100	309	100	291
		over 30	82	243	75	219	78	225
	lower	under 30	100	312	100	303	100	277
		over 30	68	198	59	184	56	171

TABLE 17
CONDITIONED VARIATION OF THE u IN Bury

sound in question	socioeconomic class of informants	contextual formality					
		informal		midformal		formal	
		%	n	%	n	%	n
vowel in bury (% mid-front lax)	upper	67	200	52	157	39	112
	middle	91	274	85	263	63	186
	lower	98	291	89	269	82	246

shows, however, linguistic environment also plays a role in determining the final sound of *potato* and *tomato* for all speakers in all contexts: when the words are followed by a consonant, schwa occurs more frequently than when they are followed by a vowel; and when the words are sentence–final, the values for schwa always occur between the values for sentence–initial and sentence–medial usages.

TABLE 18
CONDITIONED VARIATION OF THE au IN Sausage

sound in question	socioeconomic class of informants	age of informants	contextual formality: informal %	informal n	midformal %	midformal n	formal %	formal n
vowel in sausage (% low-back)	upper	under 60	100	291	100	309	100	298
		over 60	96	284	100	290	100	307
	middle	under 60	100	331	100	344	100	268
		over 60	88	169	96	183	100	301
	lower	under 60	100	319	100	344	100	326
		over 60	62	182	71	211	76	233

TABLE 19
CONDITIONED VARIATION OF THE ae IN sundae

sound in question	socioeconomic class of informants	phonetic ending	contextual formality					
			informal		midformal		formal	
			%	n	%	n	%	n
		schwa	95	1248	77	1012	64	841
	upper	[e]	0	0	10	131	19	250
		[i]	5	66	13	171	17	223
		schwa	98	1264	87	1122	72	929
<ae> in sundae	middle	[e]	0	0	0	0	6	77
		[i]	2	26	13	168	22	284
		schwa	99	1338	92	1244	78	1055
	lower	[e]	0	0	0	0	0	0
		[i]	1	14	8	108	22	297

TABLE 20
CONDITIONED VARIATION OF THE FINAL i IN Missouri

sound in question	socioeconomic class of informants	Missouri followed by	age of informants	contextual formality					
				informal		midformal		formal	
				%	n	%	n	%	n
		#C	under 30	9	29	3	10	0	0
			over 30	14	82	5	29	0	0
	upper	#V	under 30	2	4	0	0	0	0
			over 30	12	47	2	8	0	0
		##	under 30	5	29	1	3	0	0
			over 30	12	47	3	10	0	0
		#C	under 30	21	72	12	41	1	3
			over 30	30	149	18	90	4	20
final vowel in Missouri (% schwa)	middle	#V	under 30	10	30	2	6	0	0
			over 30	22	88	13	52	2	8

TABLE 20
CONDITIONED VARIATION OF THE FINAL i IN Missouri (cont.)

sound in question	socioeconomic class of informants	Missouri followed by	age of informants	contextual formality: informal %	informal n	midformal %	midformal n	formal %	formal n
		##	under 30	14	48	5	15	0	0
			over 30	25	93	14	48	2	6
		#C	under 30	43	129	29	87	13	39
			over 30	54	294	40	218	19	103
	lower	#V	under 30	28	66	15	35	8	19
			over 30	46	172	33	116	13	46
		##	under 30	34	114	20	114	9	49
			over 30	48	261	35	191	15	35

TABLE 21
CONDITIONED VARIATION OF THE FINAL o IN *potato, tomato*

sound in question	socioeconomic class of informants	potato, tomato followed by	contextual formality					
			informal		midformal		formal	
			%	n	%	n	%	n
final vowel in potato, tomato (% schwa)	upper	#C	48	125	31	85	19	51
		#V	32	87	23	63	6	18
		##	35	91	27	72	11	39
	middle	#C	77	196	54	128	39	100
		#V	51	115	36	92	28	79
		##	69	176	48	119	33	84
	lower	#C	100	250	100	236	100	241
		#V	72	189	59	148	51	131
		##	91	239	84	214	70	192

4. MORPHOLOGY AND SYNTAX

This chapter is devoted to a description of various morphological and syntactic aspects of the language of St. Louis. Under the first rubric I will discuss usages of verb forms, which, following Atwood (1953), are divided into **tense forms** (i.e., present infinitive, preterite, and past participle), **personal forms of the present indicative**, **number and concord**, **negative forms**, and **infinitives and present participles**; under the second rubric I will discuss usages of participles and prepositions. Only the general findings of my analysis will be given here; the specific raw scores for each demographic division of informants can be found in the third major section of the chapter. For the sake of convenience, the contents of each sub–section below have been alphabetized.

Morphology: Verb Forms

Tense Forms

1. BITE (past participle)

Members of the upper class almost unanimously prefer ***bitten*** to ***bit***, as do middle–class females; of the six exceptions, four are over the age of 60 and one is over 40. Middle–class males, however, except for those under 20, who also prefer ***bitten***, are more evenly divided; and lower–class speakers of both genders and all ages favor ***bit***. Females of every class and age level use ***bit*** slightly less than their male counterparts, and the use of ***bit*** also declines steadily from those over 60 to those under 20.

2. BLOW (preterite)

Standard English ***blew*** is the overwhelming favorite among most St. Louisans. Lower–class speakers over the age of 60 occasionally use ***blown***, and one elderly lower–class male reported ***blowed***.

3. BREAK (past participle)

Members of the upper class and members of the middle class up to the age of 40 use ***broken*** exclusively. Elderly middle–class females and middle–class males over 40, however, favor ***broke***, as do most members of the lower class, especially those over 20.

4. BURST (preterite)

The upper class uses only ***burst***, as do those members of the middle class under the age of 20. Usage for the rest of the middle class is nearly evenly divided between *burst* and ***bursted***, however, and the lower class overwhelmingly prefers ***bursted***, with males slightly outnumbering females.

5. BUY (past participle)

Bought is the nearly unanimous favorite among St. Louisans; only one lower–class male over the age of 60 reports using ***boughten***.

6. CATCH (preterite)

St. Louisans use ***caught*** exclusively; no other variant occurs in the language of the Gateway City.

7. CLIMB (preterite)

One lower–class male and one lower–class female, each over the age of 60, report using ***clumb***, but ***climbed*** is favored by all the other respondents. ***Clim*** was not offered as a variant.

8. COME (preterite)

Except for one male over the age of 60, who prefers ***come***, the upper class uses only ***came***. The middle class uses both ***come*** and ***came***, with men nearly evenly divided and women favoring ***came*** only slightly. Among the lower class, ***come*** prevails overwhelmingly.

9. DIVE (preterite)

Informants in every demographic cell show a clear preference for Northern ***dove***, the members of the upper class slightly more than the others. When it occurs, ***dived*** is most common in the lower class and among informants over the age of 40.

10. DO (preterite)

Members of the upper class and all members of the middle class except one female over the age of 60 use ***did***. The one exception reported ***done***, as did various members of the lower class. ***Done*** is especially strong among lower–class males over the age of 20 and among lower–class females over 60.

11. DRAG (preterite)

Although one elderly upper–class female reports ***drug***, the clear favorite among all of her peers is ***dragged***, as it is also for most members of the middle class. Members of the middle class over the age of 40, particularly males, favor ***drug*** more than do their younger middle–class counterparts, and ***drug*** also occurs sporadically among the lower class, especially when the respondents are males over 20.

12. DRAW (preterite)

Drawn occurs for one middle–class male in the 40–to–60 age group, but all of the other informants report using ***drew***. ***Drawed*** did not occur.

13. DREAM (preterite)

Both ***dreamed*** and ***dreamt*** occur in the language of St. Louis in significant numbers, though ***dreamt*** is used far more often by all classes of respondents. Among the upper class, ***dreamed*** is used by only five males and one female, and while raw scores for the use of ***dreamed*** among members of the middle class are approximately twice as high, the male:female ratio is preserved. The usage of the lower class is more evenly divided between ***dreamed*** and ***dreamt***, but only males over the age of 60 use one as often as the other.

14. DRINK (preterite)

Drank is the overwhelming St. Louis favorite, with ***drunk*** occurring only among those members of the lower class who are over the age of 60.

15. DRINK (past participle)

Most St. Louisans prefer ***drunk***, though ***drank*** occurs sporadically throughout the lower class and is used by one middle–class female aged 40 to 60.

16. DRIVE (preterite)

All St. Louisans in the survey report the Standard English ***drove***; neither ***drived***, ***driv***, nor ***driven*** appear to occur in the language of the Gateway City.

17. DRIVE (past participle)

The vast majority of respondents report ***driven***; ***drove*** occurs only occasionally among the members of the lower class, and especially among those over the age of 40.

18. DROWN (past participle)

Drowned is the almost unanimous choice among members of the upper and middle classes, with ***drownded*** occurring only infrequently in speakers over the age of 60 and once in a middle– class male aged 40 to 60. Usage among the lower class is more evenly divided, however, with females using ***drowned*** slightly more often than males of the same age. Uninflected ***drown*** does not occur in the language of St. Louis.

19. EAT (preterite)

All the informants reported using Standard English ***ate***; ***et*** was not offered as a response.

20. EAT (past participle)

Eaten is the nearly unanimous favorite among St. Louisans, with ***ate*** occurring occasionally only among those members of the lower class over the age of 40, especially males. Again (cf. # 19),***et*** was not offered as a response.

21.FIGHT (preterite)

The only variant offered in the survey was ***fought***; ***foughten*** did not occur.

22. FIT (preterite)

All demographic divisions prefer ***fit*** to ***fitted***, though that preference declines slightly from upper to lower class. When ***fitted*** does occur, it is more usual among males than females. Age does not seem to be a significant parameter by which to measure usage of this verb.

23. GIVE (preterite)

Except for middle–class males over the age of 60 and middle– class females over the age of 40, ***gave*** is standard among all members of the upper and middle classes. ***Give*** occurs regularly among speakers in the lower class, and among males slightly more than among females, though ***gave*** is still the clear favorite.

24. GROW (preterite)

St. Louisans use ***grew*** exclusively; no respondent offered ***growed*** or any other variant.

25. GROW (past participle)

Grown is the clear favorite among demographic cells, though ***grew*** occurs occasionally among members of the lower class, and especially among those over the age of 40.

26. HANG (past participle) ("the murderer was _____")

St. Louisans of all social classes and age groups overwhelmingly prefer ***hanged.*** Except for one middle–class male over the age of 60, ***hung*** does not occur at all among members of the upper and middle classes, and occurs only infrequently in lower–class speakers. When it does occur, however, it is more common among males than females.

27. HEAR (past participle)

The only variant recorded in the survey is ***heard***; no respondent offered nonstandard ***heared.***

28. HEAT (past participle)

The vast majority of St. Louisans clearly favor the Standard English ***heated***; uninflected ***heat*** occurs only occasionally among members of the lower class over the age of 60.

29. HELP (preterite)

Respondents offered only the standard ***helped***; ***holp***, ***holpen***, and other variants did not occur.

30. HELP (past participle)

Helped is again the only variant occurring in the language of St. Louis (cf. # 29).

31. KNEEL (preterite)

With the exception of one elderly middle–class female who prefers ***kneeled***, ***knelt*** occurs exclusively in the upper and middle classes. ***Knelt*** is also favored in the lower class, though ***kneeled*** occurs as well, and among older informants more often than younger ones.

32. KNIT (preterite)

The variant favored by all St. Louisans is ***knitted***; uninflected ***knit***, however, occurs sporadically among lower–class females, and especially among those over the age of 40.

33. KNOW (preterite)

Standard English ***knew*** is the most frequently–occurring variant in the survey for all demographic classes of informants. ***Known*** occurs sporadically among the lower class and among members of the middle class over the of age 40, however, with male usage slightly higher than female. One lower–class female over 60 offered ***knowed*** as her preference.

34. LEND (preterite)

Loaned and ***lent*** are both favorites among Gateway City speakers, with ***lent*** used slightly more often among members of the upper class. Members of the middle class over the age of 20 and all members of the lower class occasionally use ***lended***, though loaned ***occurs*** much more often. There appears to be no significant usage patterns according to gender.

35. LIE (present infinitive)

Usage is nearly evenly divided among the members of the upper class between ***lie*** and ***lay***, though members of the middle and especially the lower class favor ***lay***. Significant usage differences between the sexes are not discernible, but ***lay*** increases slightly in direct proportion to an increase in age.

36. LIE (preterite)

Laid is preferred by the vast makority of St. Louisans, and exclusively so among all members of the middle and lower classes except one middle–class male under the age of 20, who offered *lay*. *Lay* also occurs evenly though slightly among members of the upper class, with female usage at every age level a bit higher than male usage.

37. PLEAD (preterite)

Both *pleaded* and *pled* occur in the language of the Gateway City, though *pleaded* is the clear favorite, especially among middle–class speakers under the age of 40 and all lower–class speakers.

38. RIDE (past participle)

Ridden is favored by all members of the upper class, though both *rid* and *rode* occur occasionally among the middle class and especially the lower class. *Rid* is especially preferred by females over the age of 60 and males over 40, and *rode* was offered most often by members of both genders under 20.

39. RING (preterite)

The upper class uses *rang* exclusively. Members of the middle class use both *rang* and *rung*, with *rung* occurring only sporadically amd most often among male speakers. *Rung* is the variant favored by members of the lower class over the age of 40, especially males; those under 40 prefer *rang*.

40. RISE (preterite)

Rose is the usual form given by the respondents in all demographic cells; however, three middle–class females over the age of 40, two middle–class males over 60, and nine members of the lower class over 40 preferred *arose*. *Riz* does not occur in the language of St. Louis.

41. RUN (preterite)

One upper–class male over the age of 60 offered *run*, but the rest of the upper class uses *ran*, as do the majority of middle and lower class speakers. Regarding the independent variable of gender, middle–class males use *run* more frequently than their female counterparts, and that trend is continued among the members of the lower class as well.

42. SEE (preterite)

The upper class and female members of the middle class under the age of 40 use *saw* exclusively, with other members of the middle class also favoring *saw* but using *seen* occasionally. *Seen* also occurs regularly in the lower class, especially among males over 20, though Standard English *saw* still predominates.

43. SET (present)

Both *sit* and *set* occur frequently in the language of St. Louis, with usage so evenly divided in all demographic cells that no discernible patterns occur.

44. SET (preterite)

Set is the typical choice by members of the upper class, though nonstandard *sat* occurs consistently as well. The middle and lower classes are more evenly divided, with females of all ages in both groups showing a slight preference for *set* and males for *sat*.

45. SEW (past participle)

The strong conjugation ***sewn*** is the favorite among members of the upper and middle classes, with ***sewed*** occurring very infrequently. ***Sewed*** is the response most often given by the lower class informants, however, with male usage slightly outnumbering female.

46. SHRINK (preterite)

The upper class uses Standard English ***shrank*** almost exclusively; one upper–class female over the age of 60 reports ***shrunk***, however, which is also the usual response among the lower class. Members of the middle class have a nearly evenly divided usage, with ***shrank*** especially preferred among those under 40. No significant patterns emerge with regard to the variable of gender.

47. SIT (present)

Members of the upper and middle classes use only ***sit***, as do members of the lower class under 40. Elsewhere in the lower class, ***set*** appears slightly though consistently, and more often among males than females.

48. SIT (preterite)

Sat is the nearly unanimous response among the informants; only one lower–class male over the age of 60 reports using ***set***.

49. SNEAK (preterite)

Snuck is preferred to ***sneaked*** in all demographic cells, and is the only form reported among the upper class. ***Sneaked*** occurs occasionally among members of the middle class, especially those over the age of 40, and is also used frequently by all members of the lower class. Usage according to gender is nearly evenly divided between males and females.

50. SPOIL (past participle)

Most St. Louisans use ***spoiled*** exclusively, though ***spoilt*** occurs occasionally among members of the lower class over the age of 40, especially males.

51. STEAL (preterite)

Stoled is reported by two lower–class males over the age of 60, but elsewhere ***stole*** is the unanimous favorite. ***Stealed*** did not occur in the survey.

52. SWEAT (preterite)

Members of the upper class and male members of the middle class under the age of 40 use uninflected ***sweat*** slightly though consistently; more frequently, however, and among the other demographic cells exclusively, ***sweated*** is used.

53. SWELL (preterite)

The only members of the survey who did not report using ***swoll*** are upper–class females under the age of 40, who prefer ***swelled***. Elsewhere, ***swoll*** occurs consistently, though it displaces ***swelled*** as the favorite only among lower–class males over 40 and lower–class females over 60. Throughout the survey, more males than females in each social class and age group use ***swoll***.

54. SWELL (past participle)

Swollen is the overwhelming favorite among both the upper and the middle classes, with ***swelled*** occurring consistently though slightly. Among members of the lower class, ***swelled*** and ***swollen*** have a more even distribution, with the usual form among males over the age of 40 being ***swelled***. ***Swelled*** is consistently more popular among males for any given demographic group than among females.

55. SWIM (preterite)

The vast majority of St. Louisans prefer Standard English *swam*, though *swum* occurs occasionally among members of the lower class over the age of 60, particularly males.

56. TAKE (preterite)

Only Standard English *took* occurs in the language of St. Louis.

57. TAKE (past participle)

Taken is the only form reported among the members of the upper class, with *took* occurring infrequently in the middle class and steadily though slightly in the lower class. No definitive patterns of usage emerge with regard to the age and gender of the respondents.

58. TEACH (preterite)

The only response offered by the informants is Standard English *taught*.

59. TEAR (preterite)

Both *tore* and *torn* occur in the language of the Gateway City. *Tore* is the usual favorite in most demographic cells, though *torn* is preferred by both males and females in the lower class who are over the age of 60. *Torn* also occurs throughout the entire middle class and especially the lower class, and was further reported by two upper–class males over 60. There is a slight correlation between the use of *torn* and an increase in age of informants, and males in general use *torn* more than do females.

60.THROW (preterite)

Members of the lower class, especially those over the age of 40, occasionally report *throwed*, but elsewhere Standard English *threw* is the preferred form.

61. WAKE (preterite)

Woke is the nearly unanimous choice among all Gateway City speakers; *waked* occurs in the speech of only one lower–class female over the age of 60.

62. WEAR (past participle)

Two upper–class males over the age of 60 report *wore*, but elsewhere the upper class uses *worn* exclusively. *Wore* also occurs consistently throughout the middle and lower classes, though it displaces *worn* as the favorite only among lower–class males over 40 and lower–class females over 60.

63. WRITE (past participle)

Written is the only variant collected in the survey; *wrote* does not occur.

Personal Forms of the Present Indicative

64. BE (1st person singular)

Standard English *am* is the only variant that was offered by my informants.

65. BE (3rd person plural)

Only *are* appears to be current in the usage of St. Louisans.

66. COST (3rd person singular)

Standard English *costs* is the only form recorded in the survey.

67. DO (3rd person singular)

Does is the unanimous choice among all respondents; *do* does not occur.

68. HAVE (1st person singular)

Gateway City speakers appear to use Standard English *have* exclusively.

69. HAVE (1st person singular auxiliary) + BE

Both *I've been* and *I been* occur as variants in the pariphrastic perfect progressive verb phrase. *I've been* is strongly favored among the upper–class informants, with *I been* the lower class favorite. Usage among members of the middle class is nearly evenly divided. Males in each social class use *I been* slightly more frequently than their female counterparts; and there seems to be a slight correlation between the use of *I been* and an increase in the age of informants in all social classes.

70. MAKE (3rd person singular)

Makes alone is recorded; uninflected *make* does not occur.

71. Rinse (3rd person singular)

The unanimous favorite among all Gateway City speakers surveyed is *rinses*.

72. SAY (1st person singular)

Both *say* and *says* occur, though the latter form is restricted to the lower class, especially to those over the age of 20. There is no discernible pattern of usage regarding gender.

73. WORK (1st person singular)

The only variant offered by the respondents was Standard English *work*.

74. Work (1st person plural)

Work is again the unanimous favorite (cf. # 73); *works* does not occur.

Number and Concord

75. BE ("cabbages [+ BE]")

The unanimous choice among Gateway City speakers is Standard English *are*.

76. BE ("here [+ contracted BE] your clothes")

Both *'s* and *'re* occur frequently in the language of St. Louis. The plural form enjoys a slight preference among members of the upper class, especially females, and members of the middle class under the age of 20. Singular *'s*, however, is the form offered more often among all other demographic cells.

77. BE ("oats [+ BE]")

Only Standard English *are* occurs in the language of Gateway City speakers.

78. BE ("there [+ contracted BE] many people")

The plural form *'re* occurs among the upper class exclusively, and is also the preferred variant throughout most of the middle class. Male members of the middle class over the age of 40 and most members of the lower class, however, prefer singular *'s*.

79. BE (2nd person preterite)

Members of the upper class use *were* exclusively, though *was* occurs slightly but steadily in the middle class and is more frequent in the lower class. *Was* tends to be used by more males than females for any given age group. There seems to be no significant correlation between either of the variants and the age of the respondents, however.

80. BE (1st person plural preterite)

The upper class uses *were* exclusively, and *were* is also the favored variant for all age groups in the middle class except females over the age of 60. *Was* occurs sporadically throughout the lower class, with a higher usage reported among males and those over 40.

81. SAY (3rd person plural)

Say alone is recorded among the upper and middle classes, though *says* intrudes slightly but steadily in the lower class. The only lower class demographic cells favoring *says* over *say* are females over the age of 40 and males over 60.

82. THINK (3rd person plural)

Only Standard English ***think*** is reported among all those surveyed.

Negative Forms

83. BE + not (1st person singular)

I'm not and ***I ain't*** both occur in the language of St. Louis. Although ***ain't*** is stigmatized nationally, it still occurs occasionally among members of the upper class over the age of 60, and is used frequently by the middle class and almost exclusively by the lower class. Males typically use the nonstandard form more frequently than do females, as do older rather than younger speakers.

84. BE + not (1st person singular tag question)

When pressed for a response, many members of the middle class and nearly all of the lower class resort to ***ain't I***, and this form is offered by a few upper class informants over the age of 40 as well. Those wishing to avoid the use of ***ain't*** are nearly equally divided between ***am I not*** and ***aren't I***. Females in all demographic cells resort to the use of ***ain't I*** less often than their male counterparts. ***Amn't I*** did not occur in the survey.

85. BE + not (3rd person singular tag question)

Wasn't he is the overwhelming favorite in the language of St. Louis. ***Wan't he*** occurs only among those members of the lower class who are over the age of 40, one male of which offered ***warn't he***.

86. DARE + not (1st person singular)

The uncontracted ***dare not*** is preferred by most St. Louisans, though members of the middle and lower classes occasionally offer ***daren't***, and ***dasn't*** occurs sporadically among members of the lower class over the age of 40, especially males.

87. HAVE + not (1st person singular)

Members of the upper class use ***haven't*** exclusively, and it also occurs most frequently in the middle class. Elsewhere, however, ***ain't*** prevails. There is a slight correlation between the use of ***ain't*** and an increase in the age of the informants, though usage according to gender is too mixed to pinpoint definitive patterns.

88. OUGHT + not (3rd person singular)

Both ***oughtn't*** and Northern ***hadn't ought*** occur frequently among informants in all demographic cells. There is no discernible patterning of usage among informants according to social class, age group, or gender.

89. USED TO + not (3rd person singular)

Didn't used to is the nearly unanimous favorite among all St. Louisans, with ***usen't*** and ***usen't to*** each occurring only once among the members of the lower class over 60 years of age.

Infinitive and Present Participles

90. A + participle (present participle)

The familiar "a + participle" (e.g., ***a–working, a–running***) so common to Appalachian speech does not occur in the language of St. Louis.

91. GO (present participle)

Going is the only form recorded in the survey; *gwine* does not occur.

92. ROT (present participle)

Members of the upper class uniformly prefer Standard English *rotting*, though *rottening* occurs sporadically throughout the middle class if the informant is over the age of 40 as well as throughout the entire lower class. *Rottening* tends to be used equally by both males and females.

93. TELL (infinitive)

To tell was the unanimous response offered by the informants.

Verb Phrases

94. MIGHT COULD

Might could does not appear to occur in the language of the Gateway City.

95. WANTS IN

Wants in is very common among the respondents in all demographic cells; it occurs exclusively among the lower class and much of the middle class. Elsewhere, the unreduced *wants to come in* is the favored form. There is no significant patterning of either variant according to the age or gender of the respondents.

96. WANTS OFF

Many St. Louisans in all demographic cells use the Midlands form *wants off*, though the frequency of that usage increases in the lower class. Elsewhere, the unreduced ***wants to get off*** is the preferred form. There is no patterning according to gender, though ***wants to get off*** seems to be used more frequently as the age of the respondent decreases.

97. WANTS OUT

All of the same informants who use ***wants in*** (see # 95) also prefer ***wants out***. ***Wants to go out*** is the other common usage among St. Louisans.

Syntax: Particles and Prepositions

98. ALL ____ ONCE

The only variant occurring in the language of the Gateway City is ***at***.

99. Buttons ____ THE COAT

Only ***on*** occurs among all the respondents; no other variant was offered.

100. HALF ____ SIX

The only form recorded in the survey is ***past***; ***after*** does not occur.

101. ____ HOME

At is the preferred form by all members of all classes; ***to*** does not occur.

102. I'M NOT (____) SURE

Most St. Louisans prefer the simple ***I'm not sure***; ***I'm not for sure***, however, occurs occasionally among members of the lower class over the age of 60, and was also offered by one middle– class female between 40 and 60.

103. NAME A CHILD ____ SOMEBODY

For is the preferred form among members of the upper class and most members of the middle class, with ***after*** being the other middle–class form. Both ***after*** and ***for*** occur frequently among the members of the lower class, with ***after*** confined largely to those speakers over the age of 40.

104. QUARTER ____ THE HOUR

Northern and Southern ***to***, Midlands ***till***, and Northern ***of*** all occur in the language of St. Louis, though ***to*** is the preferred form everywhere except among the lower class. ***Of*** intrudes frequently into the usage of the upper class and infrequently among those members of the middle class under the age of 40, and ***till*** is confined largely to members of the middle class over the age of 60 and all members of the lower class. When a difference in usage according to gender occurs, men typically use ***till*** more than women.

105. ____ SICK

The almost unanimous form elicited is ***get***, though ***take*** occurs sporadically among members of the lower class over the age of 40.

106. SICK ____ THE STOMACH

To is the nearly unanimous choice among all St. Louisans. ***At*** occurs occasionally among the members of the middle class over the age of 60 and sporadically throughout the lower class except among those under 20.

107. STAND ____ ELM STREET

On is the only form recorded in the language of the Gateway City.

108. STAND ____ LINE

The only variant offered by the informants here is *in*; *on* does not occur.

109. WAIT ____ SOMEONE

Both Midlands *on* as well as *for* occur frequently. *For* is the favored term among the upper class, while the lower class prefers *on* and the middle class is nearly evenly divided. When variation according to age and gender occur, the informants who are younger and female tend to favor *for* and those who are older and male tend to favor *on*.

110. WOOD ____ THE STOVE

The only form offered by the respondents in the survey is *in*.

Specific Raw Scores for Each Demographic Division of Informants

On the following pages is given a complete list of specific raw scores for each variant recorded and for each demographic division of informants investigated. The verbs, particles, and prepositions are arranged numerically to correspond with the numbering system already employed in this chapter, and the variants of each category are listed in alphabetical order.

term	variants	upper class								middle class								lower class							
		male				female				male				female				male				female			
		< 20	20 to 40	40 to 60	60 to 80	< 20	20 to 40	40 to 60	60 to 80	< 20	20 to 40	40 to 60	60 to 80	< 20	20 to 40	40 to 60	60 to 80	< 20	20 to 40	40 to 60	60 to 80	< 20	20 to 40	40 to 60	60 to 80
1.	bit	0	0	1	2	0	0	0	1	2	4	4	5	1	0	0	1	8	9	10	10	6	8	9	9
	bitten	10	10	9	8	10	10	10	9	8	6	6	5	9	10	10	9	2	1	0	0	4	2	1	1
2.	blew	10	10	10	10	10	10	10	10	10	10	10	10	10	10	10	10	10	10	10	7	10	10	10	6
	blowed	0	0	0	0	0	0	0	0	0	0	0	0	0	0	0	0	0	0	0	1	0	0	0	0
	blown	0	0	0	0	0	0	0	0	0	0	0	0	0	0	0	0	0	0	0	2	0	0	0	4
3.	broke	0	0	0	0	0	0	0	0	0	0	6	7	0	0	0	5	4	6	6	8	3	5	5	6
	broken	10	10	10	10	10	10	10	10	10	10	4	3	10	10	10	5	6	4	4	2	7	5	5	4
4.	burst	10	10	10	10	10	10	10	10	10	6	6	5	10	5	5	4	3	2	0	0	5	3	3	1
	bursted	0	0	0	0	0	0	0	0	0	4	4	5	0	5	5	6	7	8	10	10	5	7	7	9
5.	bought	10	10	10	10	10	10	10	10	10	10	10	10	10	10	10	10	10	10	10	9	10	10	10	10
	boughten	0	0	0	0	0	0	0	0	0	0	0	0	0	0	0	0	0	0	0	1	0	0	0	0

term	variants	upper class								middle class								lower class							
		male				female				male				female				male				female			
		< 20	20 to 40	40 to 60	60 to 80	< 20	20 to 40	40 to 60	60 to 80	< 20	20 to 40	40 to 60	60 to 80	< 20	20 to 40	40 to 60	60 to 80	< 20	20 to 40	40 to 60	60 to 80	< 20	20 to 40	40 to 60	60 to 80
6.	caught	10	10	10	10	10	10	10	10	10	10	10	10	10	10	10	10	10	10	10	10	10	10	10	10
7.	climbed	10	10	10	10	10	10	10	10	10	10	10	10	10	10	10	10	10	10	10	9	10	10	10	9
	clumb	0	0	0	0	0	0	0	0	0	0	0	0	0	0	0	0	0	0	0	1	0	0	0	1
8.	came	10	10	10	9	10	10	10	10	6	5	5	4	6	6	6	5	4	3	3	1	3	3	2	2
	come	0	0	0	1	0	0	0	0	4	5	5	6	4	4	4	5	6	7	7	9	7	7	8	8
9.	dived	0	0	1	1	0	0	0	1	1	2	2	4	0	0	1	3	2	3	3	4	2	2	3	3
	dove	10	10	9	9	10	10	10	9	9	8	8	6	10	10	9	7	8	7	7	6	8	8	7	7
10.	did	10	10	10	10	10	10	10	10	10	10	10	10	10	10	10	9	8	7	4	3	9	8	7	4
	done	0	0	0	0	0	0	0	0	0	0	0	0	0	0	0	1	2	3	6	7	1	2	3	6
11.	dragged	10	10	10	10	10	10	10	9	10	8	6	7	9	10	8	9	8	5	5	4	7	6	6	6
	drug	0	0	0	0	0	0	0	1	0	2	4	3	1	0	2	1	2	5	5	6	3	4	4	4

term	variants	upper class								middle class								lower class							
		male				female				male				female				male				female			
		< 20	20 to 40	40 to 60	60 to 80	< 20	20 to 40	40 to 60	60 to 80	< 20	20 to 40	40 to 60	60 to 80	< 20	20 to 40	40 to 60	60 to 80	< 20	20 to 40	40 to 60	60 to 80	< 20	20 to 40	40 to 60	60 to 80
12.	drawn	0	0	0	0	0	0	0	0	0	0	1	0	0	0	0	0	0	0	0	0	0	0	0	0
	drew	10	10	10	10	10	10	10	10	10	10	9	10	10	10	10	10	10	10	10	10	10	10	10	10
13.	dreamed	1	2	1	1	0	0	1	0	2	2	3	3	1	1	0	1	3	4	4	5	2	3	3	4
	dreamt	9	8	9	9	10	10	9	10	8	8	7	7	9	9	10	9	7	6	6	5	8	7	7	6
14.	drank	10	10	10	10	10	10	10	10	10	10	10	10	10	10	10	10	10	10	10	7	10	10	10	10
	drunk	0	0	0	0	0	0	0	0	0	0	0	0	0	0	0	0	0	0	0	3	0	0	0	0
15.	drank	0	0	0	0	0	0	0	0	0	0	0	0	0	0	1	0	2	1	2	3	1	3	2	2
	drunk	10	10	10	10	10	10	10	10	10	10	10	10	10	10	9	10	8	9	8	7	9	7	8	8
16.	drove	10	10	10	10	10	10	10	10	10	10	10	10	10	10	10	10	10	10	10	10	10	10	10	10
17.	driven	10	10	10	10	10	10	10	10	10	10	10	10	10	10	10	10	10	8	5	5	9	9	6	5
	drove	0	0	0	0	0	0	0	0	0	0	0	0	0	0	0	0	0	2	5	5	1	1	4	5

term	variants	upper class								middle class								lower class							
		male				female				male				female				male				female			
		< 20	20 to 40	40 to 60	60 to 80	< 20	20 to 40	40 to 60	60 to 80	< 20	20 to 40	40 to 60	60 to 80	< 20	20 to 40	40 to 60	60 to 80	< 20	20 to 40	40 to 60	60 to 80	< 20	20 to 40	40 to 60	60 to 80
18.	drownded	0	0	0	1	0	0	0	0	0	0	1	2	0	0	0	1	4	3	5	6	3	3	4	5
	drowned	10	10	10	9	10	10	10	10	10	10	9	8	10	10	10	9	6	7	5	4	7	7	6	5
19.	ate	10	10	10	10	10	10	10	10	10	10	10	10	10	10	10	10	10	10	10	10	10	10	10	10
20.	ate	0	0	0	0	0	0	0	0	0	0	0	0	0	0	0	0	0	0	2	3	0	0	1	1
	eaten	10	10	10	10	10	10	10	10	10	10	10	10	10	10	10	10	10	10	8	7	10	10	9	9
21.	fought	10	10	10	10	10	10	10	10	10	10	10	10	10	10	10	10	10	10	10	10	10	10	10	10
22.	fit	9	10	10	10	10	10	10	10	9	9	8	9	10	9	10	10	8	7	7	6	8	8	8	8
	fitted	1	0	0	0	0	0	0	0	1	1	2	1	0	1	0	0	2	3	3	4	2	2	2	2
23.	gave	10	10	10	10	10	10	10	10	10	10	10	8	10	10	9	9	8	7	7	6	8	8	7	7
	give	0	0	0	0	0	0	0	0	0	0	0	2	0	0	1	1	2	3	3	4	2	2	3	3
24.	grew	10	10	10	10	10	10	10	10	10	10	10	10	10	10	10	10	10	10	10	10	10	10	10	10

		upper class								middle class								lower class							
		male				female				male				female				male				female			
term	variants	< 20	20 to 40	40 to 60	60 to 80	< 20	20 to 40	40 to 60	60 to 80	< 20	20 to 40	40 to 60	60 to 80	< 20	20 to 40	40 to 60	60 to 80	< 20	20 to 40	40 to 60	60 to 80	< 20	20 to 40	40 to 60	60 to 80
25.	grew	0	0	0	0	0	0	0	0	0	0	0	0	0	0	0	0	1	0	2	2	1	1	3	2
	grown	10	10	10	10	10	10	10	10	10	10	10	10	10	10	10	10	9	10	8	8	9	10	7	8
26.	hanged	10	10	10	10	10	10	10	10	10	10	10	9	10	10	10	10	8	9	8	7	9	10	8	8
	hung	0	0	0	0	0	0	0	0	0	0	0	1	0	0	0	0	2	1	2	3	1	0	2	2
27.	heard	10	10	10	10	10	10	10	10	10	10	10	10	10	10	10	10	10	10	10	10	10	10	10	10
28.	heat	0	0	0	0	0	0	0	0	0	0	0	0	0	0	0	0	0	0	0	2	0	0	0	1
	heated	10	10	10	10	10	10	10	10	10	10	10	10	10	10	10	10	10	10	10	8	10	10	10	9
29.	helped	10	10	10	10	10	10	10	10	10	10	10	10	10	10	10	10	10	10	10	10	10	10	10	10
30.	helped	10	10	10	10	10	10	10	10	10	10	10	10	10	10	10	10	10	10	10	10	10	10	10	10
31.	kneeled	0	0	0	0	0	0	0	0	0	0	0	0	0	0	0	1	1	2	2	3	0	0	3	4
	knelt	10	10	10	10	10	10	10	10	10	10	10	10	10	10	10	9	9	8	8	7	10	10	7	6

term	variants	upper class								middle class								lower class							
		male				female				male				female				male				female			
		< 20	20 to 40	40 to 60	60 to 80	< 20	20 to 40	40 to 60	60 to 80	< 20	20 to 40	40 to 60	60 to 80	< 20	20 to 40	40 to 60	60 to 80	< 20	20 to 40	40 to 60	60 to 80	< 20	20 to 40	40 to 60	60 to 80
32.	knit	0	0	0	0	0	0	0	0	0	0	0	0	0	0	0	0	0	0	0	0	0	1	4	3
	knitted	10	10	10	10	10	10	10	10	10	10	10	10	10	10	10	10	10	10	10	10	10	9	6	7
33.	knew	10	10	10	10	10	10	10	10	10	10	8	7	10	10	8	9	8	9	7	6	10	8	8	7
	knowed	0	0	0	0	0	0	0	0	0	0	0	0	0	0	0	0	0	0	0	0	0	0	0	1
	known	0	0	0	0	0	0	0	0	0	0	2	3	0	0	2	1	2	1	3	4	0	2	2	2
34.	lended	0	0	0	0	0	0	0	0	0	1	2	1	0	2	1	1	2	3	2	1	1	2	1	2
	lent	5	6	6	6	6	7	6	5	5	5	4	5	5	4	4	4	7	6	6	7	9	7	8	8
	loaned	5	4	4	4	4	3	4	5	5	4	4	4	5	4	5	5	1	1	2	2	0	1	1	0
35.	lay	4	5	4	6	5	5	4	5	6	7	7	8	7	7	8	9	8	9	10	10	7	7	10	10
	lie	6	5	6	4	5	5	6	5	4	3	3	2	3	3	2	1	2	1	0	0	3	3	0	0

term	variants	upper class								middle class								lower class							
		male				female				male				female				male				female			
		< 20	20 to 40	40 to 60	60 to 80	< 20	20 to 40	40 to 60	60 to 80	< 20	20 to 40	40 to 60	60 to 80	< 20	20 to 40	40 to 60	60 to 80	< 20	20 to 40	40 to 60	60 to 80	< 20	20 to 40	40 to 60	60 to 80
36.	laid	8	8	9	9	7	7	7	8	9	10	10	10	10	10	10	10	10	10	10	10	10	10	10	10
	lay	2	2	1	1	3	3	3	2	1	0	0	0	0	0	0	0	0	0	0	0	0	0	0	0
37.	pleaded	6	6	5	5	7	6	5	5	9	8	5	5	8	8	6	6	10	10	9	8	10	10	10	7
38.	rid	0	0	0	0	0	0	0	0	1	2	4	4	0	2	3	4	2	2	5	6	1	3	5	5
	ridden	10	10	10	10	10	10	10	10	7	7	6	5	9	8	6	4	5	4	3	3	7	6	4	5
	rode	0	0	0	0	0	0	0	0	2	1	0	1	1	0	1	2	3	4	2	1	2	1	1	0
39.	rang	10	10	10	10	10	10	10	10	9	8	8	7	10	9	9	9	7	6	4	3	8	7	5	4
	rung	0	0	0	0	0	0	0	0	1	2	2	3	0	1	1	1	3	4	6	7	2	3	5	6
40.	arose	0	0	0	0	0	0	0	0	0	0	0	2	0	0	1	2	0	0	2	4	0	0	2	1
	rose	10	10	10	10	10	10	10	10	10	10	10	8	10	10	9	8	10	10	8	6	10	10	8	9

term	variants	upper class								middle class								lower class							
		male				female				male				female				male				female			
		< 20	20 to 40	40 to 60	60 to 80	< 20	20 to 40	40 to 60	60 to 80	< 20	20 to 40	40 to 60	60 to 80	< 20	20 to 40	40 to 60	60 to 80	< 20	20 to 40	40 to 60	60 to 80	< 20	20 to 40	40 to 60	60 to 80
41.	ran	10	10	10	9	10	10	10	10	8	7	6	5	9	9	8	8	6	4	5	4	7	7	8	6
	run	0	0	0	1	0	0	0	0	2	3	4	5	1	1	2	2	4	6	5	6	3	3	2	4
42.	saw	10	10	10	10	10	10	10	10	9	8	8	7	10	10	9	9	8	6	6	5	8	8	9	9
	seen	0	0	0	0	0	0	0	0	1	2	2	3	0	0	1	1	2	4	4	5	2	2	1	1
43.	set	5	5	6	4	4	5	6	4	5	4	6	5	4	3	4	5	7	6	4	5	3	4	5	6
	sit	5	5	4	6	6	5	4	6	5	6	4	5	6	7	6	5	3	4	6	5	7	6	5	4
44.	sat	2	3	2	4	3	3	2	4	5	6	6	7	5	4	4	5	5	6	5	7	3	4	4	5
	set	8	7	8	6	7	7	8	6	5	4	4	3	5	6	6	5	5	4	5	3	7	6	6	5
45.	sewed	0	0	1	0	1	1	0	1	1	2	1	3	1	0	2	2	6	7	7	7	6	5	6	5
	sewn	10	10	9	10	9	9	10	9	9	8	9	7	9	10	8	8	4	3	3	3	4	5	4	5

		upper class								middle class								lower class							
		male				female				male				female				male				female			
term	variants	< 20	20 to 40	40 to 60	60 to 80	< 20	20 to 40	40 to 60	60 to 80	< 20	20 to 40	40 to 60	60 to 80	< 20	20 to 40	40 to 60	60 to 80	< 20	20 to 40	40 to 60	60 to 80	< 20	20 to 40	40 to 60	60 to 80
46.	shrank	10	10	10	10	10	10	10	9	8	7	5	5	7	7	6	5	8	7	9	10	8	8	7	9
	shrunk	0	0	0	0	0	0	0	1	2	3	5	5	3	3	4	5	2	3	1	0	2	2	3	1
47.	set	0	0	0	0	0	0	0	0	0	0	0	0	0	0	0	0	0	0	2	3	0	0	1	2
	sit	10	10	10	10	10	10	10	10	10	10	10	10	10	10	10	10	10	10	8	7	10	10	9	8
48.	sat	10	10	10	10	10	10	10	10	10	10	10	10	10	10	10	10	10	10	10	9	10	10	10	10
	set	0	0	0	0	0	0	0	0	0	0	0	0	0	0	0	0	0	0	0	1	0	0	0	0
49.	sneaked	0	0	0	0	0	0	0	0	0	1	3	4	1	1	3	3	1	1	2	3	0	2	3	3
	snuck	10	10	10	10	10	10	10	10	10	9	7	6	9	9	7	7	9	9	8	7	10	8	7	7
50.	spoiled	10	10	10	10	10	10	10	10	10	10	10	10	10	10	10	10	10	10	7	6	10	10	9	8
	spoilt	0	0	0	0	0	0	0	0	0	0	0	0	0	0	0	0	0	0	3	4	0	0	1	2

term	variants	upper class								middle class								lower class							
		male				female				male				female				male				female			
		< 20	20 to 40	40 to 60	60 to 80	< 20	20 to 40	40 to 60	60 to 80	< 20	20 to 40	40 to 60	60 to 80	< 20	20 to 40	40 to 60	60 to 80	< 20	20 to 40	40 to 60	60 to 80	< 20	20 to 40	40 to 60	60 to 80
51.	stole	10	10	10	10	10	10	10	10	10	10	10	10	10	10	10	10	10	10	10	8	10	10	10	10
	stoled	0	0	0	0	0	0	0	0	0	0	0	0	0	0	0	0	0	0	0	2	0	0	0	0
52.	sweat	3	2	2	4	2	2	2	2	1	1	0	0	0	0	0	0	0	0	0	0	0	0	0	0
	sweated	7	8	8	6	8	8	8	8	9	9	10	10	10	10	10	10	10	10	10	10	10	10	10	10
53.	swelled	9	9	8	7	10	10	9	9	8	8	6	6	9	9	9	8	6	5	3	3	7	7	6	4
	swoll	1	1	2	3	0	0	1	1	2	2	4	4	1	1	1	2	4	5	7	7	3	3	4	6
54.	swelled	2	2	1	1	1	1	1	1	2	2	3	4	1	1	1	2	4	5	6	6	4	4	4	5
	swollen	8	8	9	9	9	9	9	9	8	8	7	6	9	9	9	8	6	5	4	4	6	6	6	5
55.	swam	10	10	10	10	10	10	10	10	10	10	10	10	10	10	10	10	10	10	10	4	10	10	10	8
	swum	0	0	0	0	0	0	0	0	0	0	0	0	0	0	0	0	0	0	0	6	0	0	0	2

term	variants	upper class								middle class								lower class							
		male				female				male				female				male				female			
		< 20	20 to 40	40 to 60	60 to 80	< 20	20 to 40	40 to 60	60 to 80	< 20	20 to 40	40 to 60	60 to 80	< 20	20 to 40	40 to 60	60 to 80	< 20	20 to 40	40 to 60	60 to 80	< 20	20 to 40	40 to 60	60 to 80
56.	took	10	10	10	10	10	10	10	10	10	10	10	10	10	10	10	10	10	10	10	10	10	10	10	10
57.	taken	10	10	10	10	10	10	10	10	10	9	9	8	9	10	8	9	8	7	8	6	8	8	8	7
	took	0	0	0	0	0	0	0	0	0	1	1	2	1	0	2	1	2	3	2	4	2	2	2	3
58.	taught	10	10	10	10	10	10	10	10	10	10	10	10	10	10	10	10	10	10	10	10	10	10	10	10
59.	tore	10	10	10	8	10	10	10	10	8	7	7	5	9	8	8	7	5	5	3	2	6	6	4	3
	torn	0	0	0	2	0	0	0	0	2	3	3	5	1	2	2	3	5	5	7	8	4	4	6	7
60.	threw	10	10	10	10	10	10	10	10	10	10	10	10	10	10	10	10	9	10	7	6	9	9	8	8
	throwed	0	0	0	0	0	0	0	0	0	0	0	0	0	0	0	0	1	0	3	4	1	1	2	2
61.	waked	0	0	0	0	0	0	0	0	0	0	0	0	0	0	0	0	0	0	0	0	0	0	0	1
	woke	10	10	10	10	10	10	10	10	10	10	10	10	10	10	10	10	10	10	10	10	10	10	10	9

term	variants	upper class								middle class								lower class							
		male				female				male				female				male				female			
		< 20	20 to 40	40 to 60	60 to 80	< 20	20 to 40	40 to 60	60 to 80	< 20	20 to 40	40 to 60	60 to 80	< 20	20 to 40	40 to 60	60 to 80	< 20	20 to 40	40 to 60	60 to 80	< 20	20 to 40	40 to 60	60 to 80
62.	wore	0	0	0	2	0	0	0	0	1	2	3	3	2	2	2	3	2	3	6	6	3	3	5	6
	worn	10	10	10	8	10	10	10	10	9	8	7	7	8	8	8	7	8	7	4	4	7	7	5	4
63.	written	10	10	10	10	10	10	10	10	10	10	10	10	10	10	10	10	10	10	10	10	10	10	10	10
64.	am	10	10	10	10	10	10	10	10	10	10	10	10	10	10	10	10	10	10	10	10	10	10	10	10
65.	are	10	10	10	10	10	10	10	10	10	10	10	10	10	10	10	10	10	10	10	10	10	10	10	10
66.	costs	10	10	10	10	10	10	10	10	10	10	10	10	10	10	10	10	10	10	10	10	10	10	10	10
67.	does	10	10	10	10	10	10	10	10	10	10	10	10	10	10	10	10	10	10	10	10	10	10	10	10
68.	have	10	10	10	10	10	10	10	10	10	10	10	10	10	10	10	10	10	10	10	10	10	10	10	10
69.	I been	0	1	1	2	0	0	0	1	4	5	6	5	4	4	5	5	6	7	7	7	6	5	7	8
	I've been	10	9	9	8	10	10	10	9	6	5	4	5	6	6	5	5	4	3	3	3	4	5	3	2

term	variants	upper class								middle class								lower class							
		male				female				male				female				male				female			
		< 20	20 to 40	40 to 60	60 to 80	< 20	20 to 40	40 to 60	60 to 80	< 20	20 to 40	40 to 60	60 to 80	< 20	20 to 40	40 to 60	60 to 80	< 20	20 to 40	40 to 60	60 to 80	< 20	20 to 40	40 to 60	60 to 80
70.	makes	10	10	10	10	10	10	10	10	10	10	10	10	10	10	10	10	10	10	10	10	10	10	10	10
71.	rinses	10	10	10	10	10	10	10	10	10	10	10	10	10	10	10	10	10	10	10	10	10	10	10	10
72.	say	10	10	10	10	10	10	10	10	10	10	10	10	10	10	10	10	9	6	5	5	8	5	5	6
	says	0	0	0	0	0	0	0	0	0	0	0	0	0	0	0	0	1	4	5	5	2	5	5	4
73.	work	10	10	10	10	10	10	10	10	10	10	10	10	10	10	10	10	10	10	10	10	10	10	10	10
74.	work	10	10	10	10	10	10	10	10	10	10	10	10	10	10	10	10	10	10	10	10	10	10	10	10
75.	are	10	10	10	10	10	10	10	10	10	10	10	10	10	10	10	10	10	10	10	10	10	10	10	10
76.	’re	6	5	5	6	7	6	7	6	7	4	5	5	4	6	5	4	3	3	4	3	4	3	4	3
	’s	4	5	5	4	3	4	3	4	3	6	5	5	6	4	5	6	7	7	6	7	6	7	6	7
77.	are	10	10	10	10	10	10	10	10	10	10	10	10	10	10	10	10	10	10	10	10	10	10	10	10

term	variants	upper class								middle class								lower class							
		male				female				male				female				male				female			
		< 20	20 to 40	40 to 60	60 to 80	< 20	20 to 40	40 to 60	60 to 80	< 20	20 to 40	40 to 60	60 to 80	< 20	20 to 40	40 to 60	60 to 80	< 20	20 to 40	40 to 60	60 to 80	< 20	20 to 40	40 to 60	60 to 80
78.	're	10	10	10	10	10	10	10	10	10	8	5	4	9	8	8	8	5	4	5	3	5	5	4	3
	's	0	0	0	0	0	0	0	0	0	2	5	6	1	2	2	2	5	6	5	7	5	5	6	7
79.	was	0	0	0	0	0	0	0	0	1	2	2	2	0	1	2	1	4	3	4	2	3	4	3	3
	were	10	10	10	10	10	10	10	10	9	8	8	8	10	9	8	9	6	7	6	8	7	6	7	7
80.	was	0	0	0	0	0	0	0	0	2	1	2	3	1	3	2	5	5	4	6	7	4	4	5	6
	were	10	10	10	10	10	10	10	10	8	9	8	7	9	7	8	5	5	6	4	3	6	6	5	4
81.	say	10	10	10	10	10	10	10	10	10	10	10	10	10	10	10	10	9	8	9	4	9	9	4	4
	says	0	0	0	0	0	0	0	0	0	0	0	0	0	0	0	0	1	2	1	6	1	1	6	6
82.	think	10	10	10	10	10	10	10	10	10	10	10	10	10	10	10	10	10	10	10	10	10	10	10	10
83.	I ain't	0	0	0	2	0	0	0	1	3	4	4	6	3	5	5	5	8	7	9	10	7	9	9	9
	I'm not	10	10	10	8	10	10	10	9	7	6	6	4	7	5	5	5	2	3	1	0	3	1	1	1

term	variants	upper class								middle class								lower class							
		male				female				male				female				male				female			
		< 20	20 to 40	40 to 60	60 to 80	< 20	20 to 40	40 to 60	60 to 80	< 20	20 to 40	40 to 60	60 to 80	< 20	20 to 40	40 to 60	60 to 80	< 20	20 to 40	40 to 60	60 to 80	< 20	20 to 40	40 to 60	60 to 80
84.	ain't I	0	0	2	2	0	0	0	1	4	6	5	6	4	4	4	5	8	9	10	10	7	7	8	8
	am I not	6	6	4	3	7	4	5	5	4	2	2	2	3	3	2	3	2	1	0	0	2	1	1	2
	aren't I	4	4	4	5	3	6	5	4	2	2	3	2	3	3	4	2	0	0	0	0	1	2	1	0
85.	wan't he	0	0	0	0	0	0	0	0	0	0	0	0	0	0	0	0	0	0	0	3	0	0	1	2
	warn't he	0	0	0	0	0	0	0	0	0	0	0	0	0	0	0	0	0	0	1	0	0	0	0	0
	wasn't he	10	10	10	10	10	10	10	10	10	10	10	10	10	10	10	10	10	10	9	7	10	10	9	8
86.	dare not	10	10	10	10	10	10	10	10	10	10	8	6	10	9	8	7	10	9	6	6	9	9	8	8
	daren't	0	0	0	0	0	0	0	0	0	0	2	4	0	1	2	3	0	1	3	2	1	1	1	2
	dasn't	0	0	0	0	0	0	0	0	0	0	0	0	0	0	0	0	0	0	1	2	0	0	1	0
87.	ain't	0	0	0	0	0	0	0	0	1	2	3	3	2	2	3	2	6	7	8	8	5	6	6	8
	haven't	10	10	10	10	10	10	10	10	9	8	7	7	8	8	7	8	4	3	2	2	5	4	4	2

term	variants	upper class								middle class								lower class							
		male				female				male				female				male				female			
		< 20	20 to 40	40 to 60	60 to 80	< 20	20 to 40	40 to 60	60 to 80	< 20	20 to 40	40 to 60	60 to 80	< 20	20 to 40	40 to 60	60 to 80	< 20	20 to 40	40 to 60	60 to 80	< 20	20 to 40	40 to 60	60 to 80
88.	hadn't ought	4	5	4	6	4	3	5	6	4	5	5	5	4	3	6	5	4	3	2	2	5	4	4	2
	oughtn't	6	5	6	4	6	7	5	4	6	5	5	5	6	7	4	5	6	7	8	8	5	6	6	8
89.	didn't used to	10	10	10	10	10	10	10	10	10	10	10	10	10	10	10	10	10	10	10	9	10	10	10	9
	usen't	0	0	0	0	0	0	0	0	0	0	0	0	0	0	0	0	0	0	0	1	0	0	0	0
	usen't to	0	0	0	0	0	0	0	0	0	0	0	0	0	0	0	0	0	0	0	0	0	0	0	1
90.	a + participle	0	0	0	0	0	0	0	0	0	0	0	0	0	0	0	0	0	0	0	0	0	0	0	0
91.	going	10	10	10	10	10	10	10	0	10	10	10	10	10	10	10	10	10	10	10	10	10	10	10	10
92.	rottening	0	0	0	0	0	0	0	0	0	0	3	4	0	0	2	4	3	2	4	3	4	3	2	4
	rotting	10	10	10	10	10	10	10	10	10	10	7	6	10	10	8	6	7	8	6	7	6	7	8	6
93.	to tell	10	10	10	10	10	10	10	10	10	10	10	10	10	10	10	10	10	10	10	10	10	10	10	10
94.	might could	10	10	10	10	10	10	10	10	10	10	10	10	10	10	10	10	10	10	10	10	10	10	10	10

		upper class								middle class								lower class							
		male				female				male				female				male				female			
term	variants	< 20	20 to 40	40 to 60	60 to 80	< 20	20 to 40	40 to 60	60 to 80	< 20	20 to 40	40 to 60	60 to 80	< 20	20 to 40	40 to 60	60 to 80	< 20	20 to 40	40 to 60	60 to 80	< 20	20 to 40	40 to 60	60 to 80
95.	wants in	7	8	7	8	6	7	8	8	8	9	10	10	9	9	9	10	10	10	10	10	10	10	10	10
	...to come in	3	2	3	2	4	3	2	2	2	1	0	0	1	1	1	0	0	0	0	0	0	0	0	0
96.	wants off	4	6	6	6	3	4	6	6	4	4	5	4	5	5	4	6	7	8	9	10	8	8	9	10
	...to get off	6	4	4	4	7	6	4	4	6	6	5	6	5	5	6	4	3	2	1	0	2	2	1	0
97.	wants out	7	8	7	8	6	7	8	8	8	9	10	10	9	9	9	10	10	10	10	10	10	10	10	10
	...to go out	3	2	3	2	4	3	2	2	2	1	0	0	1	1	1	0	0	0	0	0	0	0	0	0
98.	at	10	10	10	10	10	10	10	10	10	10	10	10	10	10	10	10	10	10	10	10	10	10	10	10
99.	on	10	10	10	10	10	10	10	10	10	10	10	10	10	10	10	10	10	10	10	10	10	10	10	10
100.	past	10	10	10	10	10	10	10	10	10	10	10	10	10	10	10	10	10	10	10	10	10	10	10	10
101.	at	10	10	10	10	10	10	10	10	10	10	10	10	10	10	10	10	10	10	10	10	10	10	10	10

term	variants	upper class								middle class								lower class							
		male				female				male				female				male				female			
		< 20	20 to 40	40 to 60	60 to 80	< 20	20 to 40	40 to 60	60 to 80	< 20	20 to 40	40 to 60	60 to 80	< 20	20 to 40	40 to 60	60 to 80	< 20	20 to 40	40 to 60	60 to 80	< 20	20 to 40	40 to 60	60 to 80
102.	...for sure	0	0	0	0	0	0	0	0	0	0	0	0	0	0	1	0	0	0	0	3	0	0	0	2
	...sure	10	10	10	10	10	10	10	10	10	10	10	10	10	10	9	10	10	10	10	7	10	10	10	8
103.	after	0	0	0	0	0	0	0	0	0	0	0	2	0	0	1	1	0	1	4	5	0	0	4	3
	for	10	10	10	10	10	10	10	10	10	10	10	8	10	10	9	9	10	9	6	5	10	10	6	7
104.	of	2	3	4	4	3	4	3	5	2	0	0	0	2	1	0	0	0	0	0	0	0	0	0	0
	till	0	0	0	1	0	0	0	0	1	2	0	7	0	0	1	5	4	6	8	10	4	5	6	7
	to	8	7	6	5	7	6	7	5	7	8	10	3	8	9	9	5	6	4	2	0	6	5	4	3
105.	get	10	10	10	10	10	10	10	10	10	10	10	10	10	10	10	10	10	10	9	8	10	10	9	9
	take	0	0	0	0	0	0	0	0	0	0	0	0	0	0	0	0	0	0	1	2	0	0	1	1

term	variants	upper class								middle class								lower class							
		male				female				male				female				male				female			
		< 20	20 to 40	40 to 60	60 to 80	< 20	20 to 40	40 to 60	60 to 80	< 20	20 to 40	40 to 60	60 to 80	< 20	20 to 40	40 to 60	60 to 80	< 20	20 to 40	40 to 60	60 to 80	< 20	20 to 40	40 to 60	60 to 80
106.	at	0	0	0	0	0	0	0	0	0	0	0	2	0	0	0	1	0	2	1	1	0	1	1	2
	to	10	10	10	10	10	10	10	10	10	10	10	8	10	10	10	9	10	8	9	9	10	9	9	8
107.	on	10	10	10	10	10	10	10	10	10	10	10	10	10	10	10	10	10	10	10	10	10	10	10	10
108.	in	10	10	10	10	10	10	10	10	10	10	10	10	10	10	10	10	10	10	10	10	10	10	10	10
109.	for	7	8	6	6	8	8	7	6	4	5	4	6	5	6	5	4	3	2	3	2	5	4	2	2
	on	3	2	4	4	2	2	3	4	6	5	6	4	5	4	5	6	7	8	7	8	5	6	8	8
110.	in	10	10	10	10	10	10	10	10	10	10	10	10	10	10	10	10	10	10	10	10	10	10	10	10

5. LEXICON

The data reported in this chapter concern St. Louisans' preferences for various vocabulary items denoting commonplace things, events, or occurrances. The semantic categories used here were selected largely from those appearing in numerous other studies of lexicon, most notably Kurath (1949), and represent such general topics as foods and cooking, nature, farm and domestic animals, the home and its furnishings, terms of address, terms for members of certain minority groups, the suburban community, and a number of other miscellanesous items. Because St. Louis is a major metropolitan center and the informants used in this study are all confirmed city–dwellers, I held the number of semantic categories concerning rural life to an absolute minimum; thus all 240 informants were able to respond to every question. Although the categories are loosely grouped together according to general topic, no subheadings occur; the reader wishing to locate a specific response will need to consult the index at the end of the chapter. Finally, following the precedent set in Chapter 4, only the general findings of my analysis will be discussed here; specific raw scores for each demographic division of informants can be found in the second major section below.

Vocabulary Items

1. A SMALL, ROUND MELON WITH ORANGE FRUIT AND A TOUGH RIND

Residents of the Gateway City use ***canteloupe*** almost exclusively. One middle–class male over the age of 60 and three lower–class males over 40, however, report ***muskmelon***. ***Mushmelon*** does not occur in the language of St. Louis.

2. A STORE–BOUGHT, FRUIT–FLAVORED SPREAD FOR TOAST

Jelly is the overwhelming favorite, with ***jam*** occurring in the language of only one lower–class male over the age of 60. ***Marmelade*** is used by one upper–class female over 60 and one lower–class female between 40 and 60, and ***preserves*** occurs slightly though consistently among the middle and lower classes. No significant patterns occur with regard to the independent variables of age and gender.

3. A HOMEMADE, FRUIT–FLAVORED SPREAD FOR TOAST

Preserves occurs most often here, especially among the members of the middle and lower classes who are over the age of 40. Neither ***jam*** nor ***marmelade*** occurs at all in St. Louis, with ***jelly*** being favored by the upper class and especially the younger speakers of all classes.

4. A CHOCOLATE– OR VANILLA–FLAVORED TOPPING FOR CAKES

St. Louisans prefer ***icing*** to ***frosting***, the latter term occurring consistently though only in small numbers in most demographic divisions of informants. Gender and age of informant seem not to be important measures of usage for these lexical items.

5. CORN SERVED INTACT ON THE COB:

The nearly unanimous favorite among respondents is the Northern and North Midlands ***corn on the cob***. ***Sweet corn*** occurs only very infrequently among females in the middle class who are over the age of 60, males in the lower class over 60, and once among lower–class females aged 40 to 60.

6. YELLOW BREAD SERVED WITH BEANS AND HAM

Gateway City speakers use ***cornbread*** exclusively; no other variant occurs.

7. THICK, WHITE SUBSTANCE CONSISTING OF LARGE OR SMALL CURDS

Cottage cheese is the only term recorded in the St. Louis survey.

8. ROUND PASTRY WITH A HOLE IN THE CENTER:

The only term offered here was ***doughnut***. I did not distinguish in my description of the item between store–bought and homemade varieties, however, which may account for terms such as ***cruller*** (which I have heard used occasionally among the elderly) not occurring.

9. A DRINK MADE WITH ICE CREAM AND SODA, EATEN WITH A SPOON AND STRAW

No fewer than four variants were offered in response to this query. ***Ice cream soda*** is the clear favorite among all demographic divisions, though less so among those speakers over the age of 40. ***Ice cream float*** occurs infrequently among most groups except those under 20, who do not use it at all; it was offered most often as a response among informants between 40 and 60. ***Float*** and ***soda***, the clipped forms of the other two terms, occur only very occasionally, though never among respondents under the age of 20.

10. A TYPICAL BREAKFAST FOOD THAT IS ROUND, FLAT, AND SERVED WITH SYRUP

The vast majority of Gateway City speakers prefer ***pancakes*** here; ***hotcakes*** occurs occasionally among speakers over the age of 40, however, especially those who are members of the lower class.

11. A SMALL AMOUNT OF FOOD EATEN BETWEEN MEALS

Snack occurs exclusively among all the respondents, regardless of whether the "small amount of food" referred to includes a sandwich and drink or consists of only, for example, pretzels or peanuts.

12. A CARBONATED BEVERAGE

The overwhelming favorite among all St. Louisans is ***soda***, with ***soda pop*** a distant second. The usage of ***soda pop*** appears to increase parallel to increasing age among the informants. The clipped form ***pop*** was not offered as a variant.

13. A LARGE SANDWICH, CONTAINING A SELECTION OF MEATS AND CHEESES

Five distinct variants occur in the language of the Gateway City, with no clear favorite emerging from the data. ***Submarine*** occurs most consistently, perhaps, especially among speakers under the age of 20. ***Club*** appears at all age and social levels as well, though its use seems to dwindle somewhat as the age of informants rises. ***Poor boy*** and ***hero*** are especially popular with those respondents over 40, and the same demographic groups also occasionally favor ***dagwood***, though that usage is limited to the middle and lower classes. Between the genders, ***hero*** and ***poor boy*** tend to be favored among females, with ***club*** and ***submarine*** popular among males.

14. A KIND OF LONG BEAN

The most frequent response among all the demographic divisions of informants is the Northern and North Midlands ***string bean***; Southern and South Midlands ***green*** *bean* is used slightly though consistently, however, with its usage increasing slightly in middle–class females under the age of 60 and throughout the lower class.

15. BONE FOUND IN THE BREASTS OF FOWL

The only variant recorded in the survey is *wishbone*; neither *pulleybone* nor any other variant was offered as a response.

16. HARD, ROUND OBJECT FOUND IN THE CENTER OF CHERRIES

Southern and Midlands *seed* occurs consistently among all groups of informants, especially among the lower class, but Northern *pit* is the clear favorite among all demographic divisions except lower–class males between the ages of 20 and 40 and lower–class females over 40.

17. HARD, ROUND OBJECT FOUND IN PEACHES

The overwhelming choice among all Gateway City speakers is Southern and Midlands *seed*; *pit* occurs evenly though slightly, however, with usage increasing among members of the middle and lower classes, especially those over the age of 40.

18. THE COVERING ON AN EAR OF CORN

Most St. Louisans use the Southern and South Midlands term *shucks*, though *husks* appears consistently throughout most demographic cells, especially among those speakers over the age of 20.

19. TO REMOVE THE COVERINGS OF BEANS AND PEAS

The vast majority of St. Louisans use the Northern/Southern ***shell***, with Midlands ***hull*** occurring only infrequently among speakers over the age of 60 and three times in speakers between 40 and 60. There is no significant patterning in response according to the gender of the informant.

20. MACHINE FROM WHICH COLD WATER CAN BE DRUNK

St. Louisans under the age of 20 use ***drinking fountain*** exclusively, and it is preferred by the vast majority of other Gateway City speakers as well. ***Water cooler*** occurs elsewhere; ***water fountain*** did not appear in the survey.

21. SMALL, BROWN WOODLANDS ANIMAL WITH A STRIPE DOWN ITS BACK

Chipmunk is the only term to occur in any of the demographic cells; ***ground squirrel*** was not offered as a response.

22. SMALL, EDIBLE, FRESH–WATER CRUSTACEAN

Three variants occur, all with some frequency. ***Crawdad*** is favored among speakers in the middle and especially the lower classes, with ***crayfish*** and ***crawfish*** both popular among most members of the upper class. ***Crayfish*** is used almost exclusively among members of the upper class under 20.

23. LARGE INSECT, FREQUENTLY SEEN AROUND FRESH WATER

Dragonfly is the only term offered by those in the survey; neither ***darning needle***, ***snake doctor***, nor any other variant occurred.

24. LONG, SLIMY CREATURE SOMETIMES USED AS FISH BAIT

The overwhelming favorite here is the simple *worm*. *Earthworm* occurs infrequently among those respondents over the age of 20, particularly if they are members of the upper and middle classes, and seems strongest among females over 40.

25. SMALL INSECT THAT SOMETIMES GLOWS IN THE DARK

Firefly occurs very infrequently among those over the age of 40, but ***lightning bug*** is the clear favorite among Gateway City speakers in all demographic divisions of the survey.

26. AN EXTREMELY SMALL FISH, SOMETIMES USED FOR FISH BAIT

The unanimous response here is ***minnow***; the diminutive ***minnie*** was not offered as a response.

27. EXTREMELY LARGE WORM, OFTEN HUNTED DURING THE LATE EVENING

Nightcrawler is the only variant offered by any of the respondents in the survey.

28. SMALL, BLACK, SMELLY ANIMAL WITH A WHITE STRIPE DOWN ITS BACK

All the informants responded with Northern and North Midlands ***skunk***; ***polecat*** was not offered as a variant.

29. A SMALL RIVER OR FLOWING BODY OF FRESH WATER

The most popular response among all age groups and social levels is ***creek***; it is used exclusively by middle–class males over the age of 60, lower–class males under 20, and lower–class females between 20 and 60. ***Stream*** occurs consistently throughout the upper class and most of the middle class, and ***brook*** appears very infrequently in all social classes, especially among those respondents over 40.

30. A SUDDEN, LARGE RAIN

Downpour is the overwhelming favorite among all respondents, with ***cloudburst*** occurring sporadically throughout most demographic cells as well. No significant patterns of usage exist according to the age or gender of the speaker.

31. WHEN THERE IS A HIGH LEVEL OF WATER VAPOR IN THE AIR

The most frequently given response, especially among speakers in the upper class, is ***humid***. ***Muggy*** also occurs at all age and social levels, however, except among upper–class females under the age of 20 and lower–class females aged 20 to 40. The third response to this query, given only sporadically and especially among the middle and lower classes, is ***sticky***.

32. A KIND OF MAPLE TREE

Most St. Louisans prefer ***sugar maple***, though ***hard maple*** also occurs, especially among male members of the middle class who are over the age of 20.

33. A MALE COW

The only variant recorded among the Gateway City informants was Northern ***bull***.

34. A DOG OF UNCERTAIN LINEAGE

Both ***mutt*** and ***mongrel*** occur frequently and unpredictably in the language of St. Louis; ***mixed breed*** appears only among those informants over the age of 40, and especially among those over 60.

35. THE PLACE WHERE PIGS ARE KEPT

Pig pen is the usual response among most St. Louisans, and occurs exclusively among speakers under the age of 20 in all social levels. Elsewhere, *pig sty* appears consistently, there being a slight correlation between the increased frequency of its usage and an increase in age among informants.

36. THE SOUND A COW MAKES

The Northern and North Midlands *moo* is the only term offered by all respondents; *low* did not appear in the survey.

37. A MALE SHEEP

The unanimous favorite among all Gateway City speakers is *ram*.

38. THE SOUND A HORSE MAKES

The unanimous response by all informants under the age of 20 is *neigh*, and it is the popular favorite elsewhere as well. *Whinny* occurs occasionally and consistently among speakers over 40.

39. A COVERING FOR WINDOWS; CAN BE RAISED AND LOWERED

Blinds is the only term offered by any of the respondents in the survey.

40. A PIECE OF FURNITURE USED TO STORE CLOTHES

Chest of drawers is the most frequently occurring variant; it occurs exclusively among upper– and middle–class females over the age of 60 and among lower–class females between 40 and 60. *Dresser* also occurs regularly among those respondents under 40 and especially among those under 20. *Bureau* appears only very occasionally, occurring four times in the language of those people over 60 and once in the language of an upper–class female aged 40 to 60.

41. A PLACE BUILT INTO THE WALL AND USED TO STORE HANGING CLOTHES

Simple *closet* is the nearly unanimous favorite among Gateway City speakers of all ages and social levels; however, *clothes closet* occurs sporadically throughout those informants over the age of 60 and once in the language of a middle–class female aged 40 to 60.

42. VEHICLE USED FOR GUIDING SMOKE FROM THE FIREPLACE TO THE OUTDOORS

Chimney is the overwhelming response here, though *flue* also occurs regularly, especially among those respondents over the age of 40.

43. A CONTAINER MADE OF METAL AND USED TO CARRY WATER

Northern and Northern Midlands *pail* occurs in the language of only one upper–class male over the age of 60 and one upper–class female aged 40 to 60; elsewhere, *bucket* occurs exclusively.

44. A CONTAINER MADE OF WOOD AND USED TO CARRY WATER

Only the Southern and South Midlands term *bucket* occurs in the language of St. Louis.

45. TO DUST AND STRAIGHTEN UP THE HOUSE

The nearly unanimous choice here is ***clean up***. ***Tidy up*** appears only infrequently, and never among those speakers under the age of 20. Neither ***redd up*** nor ***ridd up*** was offered as a variant.

46. A WEB KNOWN TO HAVE BEEN MADE BY A SPIDER

Spider web occurs exclusively in the language of the Gateway City.

47. A WEB KNOWN TO HAVE BEEN FORMED FROM DUST

Both ***cobweb*** and ***spiderweb*** appear, with no discernible patterns of usage according to the social class, age, or gender of the respondents.

48. A WEB OF UNCERTAIN ORIGINS

Cobweb is the usual response, though ***spider web*** occurs frequently and consistently as well. ***Spider web*** appears to be favored by those respondents under the age of 20 in all social classes and both genders.

49. DUST THAT COLLECTS UNDER THE BED

Simple ***dust*** is the nearly unanimous favorite among all Gateway City speakers. ***Lint*** occurs occasionally among speakers of all social classes and both genders over the age of 40, and ***dustballs*** was offered by two upper–class females aged 20 to 40, one middle–class female under 20, and one lower–class male between 20 and 40.

50. INDOOR WATER RECEPTACLE

Only ***faucet*** was recorded in the survey; ***spiggot*** and other variants did not occur.

51. OUTDOOR WATER RECEPTACLE

The unanimous choice among those surveyed is again *faucet* (cf. # 50).

52. A METAL CONTAINER USED TO PREPARE FOOD ON THE STOVE

Frying pan is clearly the favorite among respondents in all demographic divisions, though *skillet* occurs consistently in speakers over the age of 40 in both genders and all socioeconomic levels.

53. LARGE ROOM USED FOR RELAXING AND ENTERTAINING

The nearly unanimous choice is *living room*; *front room* occurs only occasionally among respondents over the age of 40 in the upper and middle classes.

54. USED TO CHANNEL WATER OFF THE ROOF OF THE HOUSE

Water troughs occurs among speakers of all social classes over the age of 60 and sporadically among those aged 40 to 60, but *gutters* is the unanimous choice of all other Gateway City speakers.

55. A BATHROOM LOCATED OUTDOORS

Most frequently occurring in the language of St. Louis is the Northern term *outhouse*; it is used by members of the lower class and all speakers under the age of 20 exclusively. *Privy* appears infrequently among members of the upper and middle classes over the age of 60, and *outdoor toilet* was offered by twelve members of the upper class between 20 and 60.

56. PART OF THE HOUSE EXTENDING BEYOND THE FRONT DOOR

Front porch is the term collected among the upper and middle classes, though *stoop* intrudes regularly into the language of the lower class at all age levels. There is no significant patterning according to the gender of the informants.

57. PART OF THE BASEMENT WHERE FRUITS AND VEGETABLES ARE STORED

Although *root cellar* occurs regularly but slightly in all demographic cells except for those containing informants under the age of 20, and appears to be especially strong in speakers over 60, *cellar* is by far the favorite in the language of St. Louis.

58. LARGE KITCHEN APPLIANCE USED TO STORE COLD FOOD

Refrigerator is used by at least half the informants in all demographic divisions, though it never occurs exclusively. The clipped *fridge* occurs regularly in all social classes and most age groups, but is especially popular among upper–class informants under the age of 40. Members of the upper class over 40 and several members of the middle and lower classes at all age levels prefer *icebox*.

59. PIECE OF FURNITURE ON WHICH SEVERAL PEOPLE CAN SIT AT ONCE

The vast majority of St. Louisans use *couch*; *sofa* intrudes only among the females of all social classes. *Davenport*, *chesterfield*, and other variants do not occur in the language of the Gateway City.

60. USED TO SUPPORT WOOD WHILE IT IS BEING CUT

Sawhorse appears most frequently among members of all social classes and both genders who are under the age of 40, and *sawbuck* was offered by informants over 40, especially males.

61. PAPER CONTAINER IN WHICH GROCERIES AND OTHER THINGS ARE CARRIED

Both ***paper bag*** and ***bag*** occur frequently and consistently in the language of St. Louis, though the clipped form is a bit more common. ***Sack*** appears only sporadically among the members of the middle and lower classes.

62. INDOOR RECEPTACLE FOR REFUSE:

Both ***trash can*** and ***waste can*** occur in the language of St. Louis, but there are no significant patterns of usage according to any of the independent variables used in this study.

63. OUTDOOR RECEPTACLE FOR REFUSE

Trash can is the overwhelming favorite in all demographic cells, and is used by those informants under the age of 20 exclusively. Elsewhere, and especially among those speakers over 60, ***garbage can*** occurs.

64. TERM OF ADDRESS FOR THE MALE PARENT

The nearly unanimous favorite is ***dad***, though both ***father*** and ***daddy*** occur sporadically. ***Father*** is restricted to usage by males between the ages of 20 and 60, ***daddy*** to usage by females under 40.

65. TERM OF ADDRESS FOR THE FEMALE PARENT

Mom is the preferred variant in all demographic cells, with ***mother*** occurring occasionally among respondents aged 20 to 60 and ***mommy*** appearing once each in the speech of upper– and middle–class females under 20.

66. PEJORATIVE TERM FOR A WHITE PERSON

Hillbilly occurs in the speech of one middle–class female over the age of 60, but the popular favorite in all other demographic cells is ***hoosier***.

67. NEUTRAL TERM FOR A BLACK PERSON

The term favored among most isformants is ***black***; it is used exclusively by all speakers under 20. A common form elsewhere is ***negro***, with ***spook***, ***colored***, ***coon***, and ***nigger*** all occurring very infrequently and unpredictably among the three social classes. There appears to be no patterning of these variants according to the gender of the informants.

68. PEJORATIVE TERM FOR A BLACK PERSON

The two favorites in this semantic category are ***hoosier*** and ***nigger***: ***hoosier*** is preferred most often by members of the upper class except males between the ages of 20 and 40, middle–class males over 40 and middle–class females aged 20 to 40 and 60 to 80, and all members of the lower class except males under 40; ***nigger*** is used consistently by upper–class males between 20 and 40, middle–class males under 40 and middle–class females under 20 and 40 to 60, and lower–class males under 40. ***Spook*** is used infrequently by members of each gender and socioeconomic class, ***hillbilly*** is reported by one middle–class male aged 60 to 80, and ***coon*** is favored by one middle–class and two lower–class males over the age 40.

69. TERM FOR A MEMBER OF THE POLICE FORCE

Four variants occur in the language of St. Louis. ***Policeman*** and ***cop*** are both the usual responses, each occurring regularly in all demographic cells. ***Fuzz*** is offered by one middle–class male aged 20 to 40, and ***pig*** is preferred by three members of the lower class under 40.

70. TERM FOR MEMBERS OF THE EXTENDED FAMILY

The nearly unanimous favorite among Gateway City speakers in all demographic cells is ***relatives***; ***relations*** occurs in the speech of only one upper–class male over the age of 60.

71. TERM OF ADDRESS FOR A GROUP OF PEOPLE, MALE AND FEMALE

Both ***guys*** and ***you guys*** occur frequently and regularly in all demographic divisions of the survey. ***Youse guys*** was offered only by two males aged 40 to 60, one each from the upper and lower classes.

72. BUILDING WHERE THE FIRE ENGINES ARE STORED

Fire house and ***fire station*** receive almost equal use in the language of St Louis, though ***fire house*** is the preferred form. There are no discernible patterns of usage regarding social class, age, or gender.

73. WHERE THE FIREMEN ATTACH THE HOSE TO OBTAIN WATER

Three terms are popular in St. Louis. ***Fire hydrant*** is the most frequent response for informants over the age of 40, though it occurs regularly in the other demographic cells as well. ***Fire plug*** occurs steadily but slightly throughout the language of the Gateway City, but is especially favored by middle–class males over the age of 60. Elsewhere, and particularly among respondents under 40, ***hydrant*** is the preferred form.

74. PIECE OF PLAYGROUND EQUIPMENT USED BY TWO CHILDREN AT ONCE

Seesaw is the typical response, and the only one offered by all informants under the age of 20 and most under 40. ***Teeter totter*** occurs occasionally among those members of all social classes who are over 40. No patterning of these variants occurs according to the gender of the informants.

75. LARGEST KIND OF OVER–THE–ROAD TRUCK

No fewer than four variants were offered here. ***Semi*** and ***MAC truck*** occur sporadically throughout all the demographic categories, but are more popular among speakers aged 20 to 60; speakers over 60 typically prefer ***tractor–trailer***; and those under 20 use ***eighteen–wheeler***. No demographic division of informants uses a term to the exclusion of any other, and no discernible patterns occur regarding gender and social class.

76. PLACE WHERE TRUCKS ARE LOADED AND UNLOADED

Most participants in the survey use ***dock***; upper–class males over the age of 60 and lower–class males aged 20 to 40 use it exclusively. Elsewhere, ***pier*** receives consistent though slight use, and ***wharf*** was offered by one respondent between 60 and 80 in each socioeconomic class.

77. A RIDE DOWNHILL ON A SLED, LYING ON THE STOMACH

The Northern and North Midlands term ***belly buster*** is the typical response among the vast majority of people in all demographic cells, ***belly bumper*** occurs slightly though consistently, and ***belly flop*** was offered by two females over the age of 60, one each from the upper and lower classes.

78. WHEN ONE DIVING INTO A POOL OR LAKE LANDS ON HIS OR HER STOMACH

Belly flop is used exclusively among upper– and middle–class respondents under the age of 20, and occurs most frequently in all other demographic cells as well. Elsewhere, ***belly buster*** occurs consistently, especially among males. No other variant was offered as a response.

79. TO SUDDENLY EXPEL GAS THROUGH THE MOUTH

Both ***burp*** and ***belch*** occur in the language of the Gateway City, with ***burp*** occurring slightly more often in the upper class and ***belch*** in the middle and lower classes. Between the genders, females seem to favor ***burp*** and males ***belch***. There is no discernible pattern of usage regarding the age of the informants.

80. USED TO DESCRIBE SOMETHING ON THE DIAGONAL PLANE

Catty–corner is the nearly unanimous response among all St. Louisans in the survey; ***kitty–corner*** occurs only among two lower–class males over the age of 60.

81. TO GO WITH SOMEONE SOMEWHERE, AS A MAN AND WOMAN ON A DATE

Although ***escort*** was offered by eight upper–class females over the age of 60, the popular favorite in all other demographic cells was ***take***.

82. FOR A CHILD AND A PARENT TO HAVE PHYSICAL FEATURES IN COMMON

No fewer than four variants occur for this term. ***Favors*** was preferred by only three members of the middle class between the ages of 40 and 60 and seven members of the lower class over 40. Both ***resembles*** and ***looks*** like are consistent favorites in all demographic cells, though ***looks like*** occurs much more often. Most members of the middle and lower classes also show a preference for ***takes after***, though it displaces all other variants only among members of the lower class aged 20 to 40.

83. WHEN A BABY MOVES ON ALL FOURS

The only variant occurring among the informants interviewed was the Southern and Midlands term ***crawl.***

84. WHEN AN ADULT BABYSITS A CHILD OR INFANT

The overwhelming favorite among most St. Louisans is ***take care of***, though ***look after*** was reported by two lower–class males over the age of 60 and five lower–class females over 40.

85. WHEN PARENTS NURTURED A CHILD TO ADULTHOOD

Brought up occurs sporadically among members of the lower class over the age of 40, but ***raised*** is the unanimous favorite elsewhere.

86. WHEN A CHILD INTENTIONALLY MISSES SCHOOL

Five variants occur in the language of ST. Louis. The unanimous favorite among those informants under the age of 20 is ***skip***, and it occurs throughout most other demographic cells as well, though slightly. ***Skip school*** is used the most by members of all social classes aged 20 to 40, though Northern and North Midlands ***play hookey*** is the most popular form for all respondents over 20. ***Skip class*** was offered sporadically by members of all social classes aged 20 to 60. No discernible patterns occur regarding gender with the exception of females using ***be truant*** more often than males. ***Bag school/class*** was not offered as a variant by any of the respondents.

87. FAR AWAY OR FAR TO GO

Long ways is the most typical response among residents in all the demographic cells; it is used exclusively by middle–class females over the age of 60. Elsewhere, however, ***long way*** is the preferred form.

88. WHEN A ROAD IS WET OR ICY

Both ***slick*** and ***slippery*** occur frequently in the language of St. Louis, with ***slippery*** the slight favorite among members of the upper class and more often offered by members of the lower class. Among members of the middle class, both forms occur with nearly equal frequency. None of the variants appears to pattern according to the gender or age of the informants.

89. MAGNIFYING GLASSES USED AT SPORTING EVENTS, ETC.

Usage here is delineated strongly according to the age of the informants. Those under 40 typically prefer ***binoculars***; all but one lower–class male under 20 use it exclusively. Among those respondents over 40, however, ***fieldglasses*** makes a very strong showing.

90. WHAT A DEAD PERSON IS BURIED IN

Both ***casket*** and ***coffin*** occur in the language of St. Louis. ***Coffin*** is the preferred form among most members of the upper and middle classes, especially females, with other respondents typically offering ***casket***. Usage among all demographic cells, however, is fairly evenly divided.

91. WHEN THE CAR RECEIVES LUBRICATION

Members if the upper class typically have their cars ***greased***, and while that term occurs in all the other demographic cells as well, members of the middle and lower classes prefer ***grease job***. ***Lube job*** occurs sporadically among members of the lower class over 20, though the clipped ***lube*** was not offered as a variant.

92. A SMALL, MELODIOUS MUSICAL INSTRUMENT PLAYED AROUND CAMPFIRES

The nearly unanimous favorite among St. Louisans in all the demographic cells studied is ***harmonica***, though ***mouth harp*** was offered by one lower–class male between the ages of 40 and 60 and occurs regularly though slightly among members of all social classes over 60 as well.

93. WHAT A BABY IS WHEELED AROUND THE NEIGHBORHOOD IN

Midlands ***baby buggy*** is the term used exclusively among those informants under the age of 40; it also occurs as the most popular form elsewhere. Respondents over 40, however, sometimes prefer ***carriage*** and ***baby carriage***, both of which occur regularly though slightly. ***Pram*** did not occur in the survey.

94. WHAT A MAN WEARS WHILE SWIMMING

Most of the respondents in the survey offered ***swim suit***; in fact, all informants under the age of 20 except one lower–class female use it exclusively. Elsewhere, ***swim trunks*** occurs consistently; and ***bathing suit*** was offered by several upper– and middle–class females over 40.

95. USED BY CHILDREN ON SNOWY HILLS

Sled is the most frequently occurring form here, with ***sleigh*** occurring slightly but regularly in most demographic cells. There is no discernible pattern regarding usage and the social class, age, or gender of the informants.

96. TERM FOR AN APPARITION

The nearly unanimous favorite among Gateway City speakers is ***ghost***; ***spook*** was offered by only one lower–class male over the age of 60.

Specific Raw Scores For Each Demographic Division Of Informants

On the following pages is given a complete list of specific raw scores for each variant recorded and for each demographic division of informants investigated. The lexical items are arranged numerically to correspond with the numbering system already employed in this chapter, and the variants of each semantic category are listed in alphabetical order.

		upper class								middle class								lower class							
		male				female				male				female				male				female			
term	variants	< 20	20 to 40	40 to 60	60 to 80	< 20	20 to 40	40 to 60	60 to 80	< 20	20 to 40	40 to 60	60 to 80	< 20	20 to 40	40 to 60	60 to 80	< 20	20 to 40	40 to 60	60 to 80	< 20	20 to 40	40 to 60	60 to 80
1.	cantaloupe	10	10	10	10	10	10	10	10	10	10	10	9	10	10	10	10	10	10	9	8	10	10	10	10
	muskmelon	0	0	0	0	0	0	0	0	0	0	0	1	0	0	0	0	0	0	1	2	0	0	0	0
2.	jam	0	0	0	0	0	0	0	0	0	0	0	0	0	0	0	0	0	0	0	1	0	0	0	0
	jelly	10	10	10	10	10	10	10	9	10	8	7	7	10	9	8	8	8	9	10	7	8	8	6	7
	marmelade	0	0	0	0	0	0	0	1	0	0	0	0	0	0	0	0	0	0	0	0	0	0	1	0
	preserves	0	0	0	0	0	0	0	0	0	2	3	3	0	1	2	2	2	1	0	2	2	2	4	3
3.	jelly	9	8	8	7	10	7	7	8	7	4	5	3	2	5	4	4	3	6	5	2	2	3	1	2
	preserves	1	2	2	3	0	3	3	2	3	6	5	7	8	5	6	6	7	4	5	8	8	7	9	8
4.	frosting	2	3	3	3	1	2	0	2	2	1	3	2	1	0	2	4	2	1	2	2	3	2	1	3
	icing	8	7	7	7	9	8	10	8	8	9	7	8	9	10	8	6	8	9	8	8	7	8	9	7

	term variants	upper class								middle class								lower class							
		male				female				male				female				male				female			
		< 20	20 to 40	40 to 60	60 to 80	< 20	20 to 40	40 to 60	60 to 80	< 20	20 to 40	40 to 60	60 to 80	< 20	20 to 40	40 to 60	60 to 80	< 20	20 to 40	40 to 60	60 to 80	< 20	20 to 40	40 to 60	60 to 80
5.	corn...cob	10	10	10	10	10	10	10	10	10	10	10	10	10	10	10	8	10	10	10	7	10	10	9	10
	sweet corn	0	0	0	0	0	0	0	0	0	0	0	0	0	0	0	2	0	0	0	3	0	0	1	0
6.	cornbread	10	10	10	10	10	10	10	10	10	10	10	10	10	10	10	10	10	10	10	10	10	10	10	10
7.	cottage cheese	10	10	10	10	10	10	10	10	10	10	10	10	10	10	10	10	10	10	10	10	10	10	10	10
8.	doughnut	10	10	10	10	10	10	10	10	10	10	10	10	10	10	10	10	10	10	10	10	10	10	10	10
9.	float	0	0	0	1	0	0	0	1	0	0	0	2	0	1	1	0	0	0	2	3	0	1	1	1
	ice cream float	0	1	2	1	0	0	2	0	0	0	4	1	0	0	0	1	0	1	4	0	0	0	2	1
	ice cream soda	10	9	7	7	10	10	8	9	10	10	6	5	10	9	8	8	10	7	4	5	10	8	5	6
	soda	0	0	1	1	0	0	0	0	0	0	0	2	0	0	1	1	0	2	0	2	0	1	2	2
10.	hot cakes	0	0	0	1	0	0	0	0	0	0	1	2	0	0	0	1	0	0	3	3	0	0	2	1
	pancakes	10	10	10	9	10	10	10	10	10	10	9	8	10	10	10	9	10	10	7	7	10	10	8	9

term	variants	upper class								middle class								lower class							
		male				female				male				female				male				female			
		< 20	20 to 40	40 to 60	60 to 80	< 20	20 to 40	40 to 60	60 to 80	< 20	20 to 40	40 to 60	60 to 80	< 20	20 to 40	40 to 60	60 to 80	< 20	20 to 40	40 to 60	60 to 80	< 20	20 to 40	40 to 60	60 to 80
11.	snack	10	10	10	10	10	10	10	10	10	10	10	10	10	10	10	10	10	10	10	10	10	10	10	10
12.	soda	9	10	8	7	10	9	7	6	9	8	7	8	10	8	7	8	10	9	9	8	9	8	7	6
	soda pop	1	0	2	3	0	1	3	4	1	2	3	2	0	2	3	2	0	1	1	2	1	2	3	4
13.	club	4	2	1	0	3	4	2	3	2	3	1	0	4	2	0	1	3	3	2	1	3	4	1	0
	dagwood	0	0	0	0	0	0	0	0	0	0	2	3	0	0	1	3	0	0	3	4	0	0	2	3
	hero	1	3	2	3	0	2	1	1	1	1	2	3	1	2	1	2	2	2	3	3	0	2	3	2
	poor boy	2	2	4	5	1	1	3	2	0	2	2	2	1	3	3	4	0	1	1	2	0	1	2	2
	submarine	3	3	3	2	6	3	4	4	7	4	3	2	4	3	5	0	5	4	1	0	7	3	2	3
14.	green bean	2	3	1	0	1	1	0	0	2	1	0	1	4	2	3	1	5	4	2	1	2	2	1	2
	string bean	8	7	9	10	9	9	10	10	8	9	10	9	6	8	7	9	5	6	8	9	8	8	9	8
15.	wishbone	10	10	10	10	10	10	10	10	10	10	10	10	10	10	10	10	10	10	10	10	10	10	10	10

		upper class								middle class								lower class							
		male				female				male				female				male				female			
term	variants	< 20	20 to 40	40 to 60	60 to 80	< 20	20 to 40	40 to 60	60 to 80	< 20	20 to 40	40 to 60	60 to 80	< 20	20 to 40	40 to 60	60 to 80	< 20	20 to 40	40 to 60	60 to 80	< 20	20 to 40	40 to 60	60 to 80
16.	pit	7	6	8	7	9	8	8	7	6	7	7	6	7	8	6	6	6	5	6	6	7	6	5	5
	seed	3	4	2	3	1	2	2	3	4	3	3	4	3	2	4	4	4	5	4	4	3	4	5	5
17.	pit	1	2	2	3	0	1	1	2	2	2	3	3	1	2	3	3	2	3	4	4	2	2	3	2
	seed	9	8	8	7	10	9	9	8	8	8	7	7	9	8	7	7	8	7	6	6	8	8	7	8
18.	husks	1	2	2	1	0	1	3	2	1	3	2	3	1	0	2	3	0	1	2	2	0	2	1	3
	shucks	9	8	8	9	10	9	7	8	9	7	8	7	9	10	8	7	10	9	8	8	10	8	9	7
19.	hull	0	0	1	3	0	0	0	2	0	0	0	3	0	0	0	1	0	0	0	4	0	0	2	3
	shell	10	10	9	7	10	10	10	8	10	10	10	7	10	10	10	9	10	10	10	6	10	10	8	7
20.	drink. fount.	10	9	10	8	10	8	9	8	10	9	9	8	10	8	7	9	10	9	10	9	10	8	9	7
	water cooler	0	1	0	2	0	2	1	2	0	1	1	2	0	2	3	1	0	1	0	1	0	2	1	3
21.	chipmunk	10	10	10	10	10	10	10	10	10	10	10	10	10	10	10	10	10	10	10	10	10	10	10	10

	term variants	upper class								middle class								lower class							
		male				female				male				female				male				female			
		< 20	20 to 40	40 to 60	60 to 80	< 20	20 to 40	40 to 60	60 to 80	< 20	20 to 40	40 to 60	60 to 80	< 20	20 to 40	40 to 60	60 to 80	< 20	20 to 40	40 to 60	60 to 80	< 20	20 to 40	40 to 60	60 to 80
22.	crawdad	2	2	2	3	1	0	1	2	5	6	5	6	4	5	6	5	8	9	6	8	6	7	7	7
	crawfish	1	6	6	5	1	7	6	5	3	3	3	3	3	2	3	2	1	3	1	3	3	3	2	3
	crayfish	7	2	2	2	8	3	2	3	0	1	2	1	3	2	2	2	0	0	1	1	1	0	1	0
23.	dragonfly	10	10	10	10	10	10	10	10	10	10	10	10	10	10	10	10	10	10	10	10	10	10	10	10
24.	earthworm	0	0	1	1	0	1	2	4	0	0	1	1	0	1	2	4	0	0	0	0	0	0	1	0
	worm	10	10	9	9	10	9	8	6	10	10	9	9	10	9	8	6	10	10	10	10	10	10	9	10
25.	firefly	0	0	1	2	0	0	1	1	0	0	0	1	0	1	0	1	0	0	0	0	0	0	1	1
	lightning bug	10	10	9	8	10	10	9	9	10	10	10	9	10	9	10	9	10	10	10	10	10	10	9	9
26.	minnow	10	10	10	10	10	10	10	10	10	10	10	10	10	10	10	10	10	10	10	10	10	10	10	10
27.	night crawler	10	10	10	10	10	10	10	10	10	10	10	10	10	10	10	10	10	10	10	10	10	10	10	10
28.	skunk	10	10	10	10	10	10	10	10	10	10	10	10	10	10	10	10	10	10	10	10	10	10	10	10

	term variants	upper class								middle class								lower class							
		male				female				male				female				male				female			
		< 20	20 to 40	40 to 60	60 to 80	< 20	20 to 40	40 to 60	60 to 80	< 20	20 to 40	40 to 60	60 to 80	< 20	20 to 40	40 to 60	60 to 80	< 20	20 to 40	40 to 60	60 to 80	< 20	20 to 40	40 to 60	60 to 80
29.	brook	0	0	1	2	0	0	1	1	0	0	0	0	1	0	1	1	0	1	1	0	1	0	0	0
	creek	6	7	6	6	7	8	7	6	8	9	8	10	9	8	7	8	10	9	8	9	9	10	10	9
	stream	4	3	3	2	3	2	2	3	2	1	2	0	0	2	2	1	0	0	1	1	0	0	0	1
30.	cloudburst	1	2	1	0	0	1	1	1	2	0	1	2	1	0	2	3	1	2	0	1	0	0	1	2
	downpour	9	8	9	10	10	9	9	9	8	10	9	8	9	10	8	7	9	8	10	9	10	10	9	8
31.	humid	8	8	9	7	10	9	7	6	9	7	6	6	8	7	6	5	8	8	7	6	8	9	7	5
	muggy	2	1	1	1	0	1	2	2	1	1	3	2	2	1	3	3	1	2	3	2	1	0	2	2
32.	hard maple	0	1	2	2	0	1	2	2	0	2	3	4	0	1	2	1	0	2	2	1	0	1	1	2
	sugar maple	10	9	8	8	10	9	8	8	10	8	7	6	10	9	8	9	10	8	8	9	10	9	9	8
33.	bull	10	10	10	10	10	10	10	10	10	10	10	10	10	10	10	10	10	10	10	10	10	10	10	10

	term variants	upper class								middle class								lower class							
		male				female				male				female				male				female			
		< 20	20 to 40	40 to 60	60 to 80	< 20	20 to 40	40 to 60	60 to 80	< 20	20 to 40	40 to 60	60 to 80	< 20	20 to 40	40 to 60	60 to 80	< 20	20 to 40	40 to 60	60 to 80	< 20	20 to 40	40 to 60	60 to 80
34.	mixed breed	0	0	0	1	0	0	1	2	0	0	0	1	0	0	0	1	0	0	1	1	0	0	0	2
	mongrel	4	3	4	4	3	2	1	2	5	4	5	2	4	5	6	4	4	5	2	4	4	3	5	2
	mutt	6	7	6	5	7	8	8	6	5	6	5	7	6	5	4	5	6	5	7	5	6	7	5	6
35.	pig pen	10	8	6	5	10	9	7	6	10	8	8	5	10	9	9	4	10	8	6	5	10	9	8	7
	pig sty	0	2	4	5	0	1	3	4	0	2	2	5	0	1	1	6	0	2	4	5	0	1	2	3
36.	moo	10	10	10	10	10	10	10	10	10	10	10	10	10	10	10	10	10	10	10	10	10	10	10	10
37.	ram	10	10	10	10	10	10	10	10	10	10	10	10	10	10	10	10	10	10	10	10	10	10	10	10
38.	neigh	10	9	7	8	10	8	6	7	10	8	7	8	10	9	7	6	10	8	7	7	10	7	6	5
	whinny	0	1	3	2	0	2	4	3	0	2	3	2	0	1	3	4	0	2	3	3	0	3	4	5
39.	blinds	10	10	10	10	10	10	10	10	10	10	10	10	10	10	10	10	10	10	10	10	10	10	10	10

	term variants	upper class								middle class								lower class							
		male				female				male				female				male				female			
		< 20	20 to 40	40 to 60	60 to 80	< 20	20 to 40	40 to 60	60 to 80	< 20	20 to 40	40 to 60	60 to 80	< 20	20 to 40	40 to 60	60 to 80	< 20	20 to 40	40 to 60	60 to 80	< 20	20 to 40	40 to 60	60 to 80
40.	bureau	0	0	0	1	0	0	1	0	0	0	0	1	0	0	0	0	0	0	0	1	0	0	0	1
	chest of draw.	5	6	8	7	4	7	8	10	5	5	7	8	5	6	9	10	4	8	6	7	3	8	10	9
	dresser	5	4	2	2	6	3	1	0	5	5	3	1	5	4	1	0	6	2	4	2	7	2	0	1
41.	closet	10	10	10	9	10	10	10	8	10	10	10	9	10	10	9	9	10	10	10	9	10	10	10	8
	clothes closet	0	0	0	1	0	0	0	2	0	0	0	1	0	0	1	1	0	0	0	1	0	0	0	2
42.	chimney	10	9	7	6	9	9	7	7	10	8	8	5	9	9	9	6	10	10	6	5	8	7	5	5
	flue	0	1	3	4	1	1	3	3	0	2	2	5	1	1	1	4	0	0	4	5	2	3	5	5
43.	bucket	10	10	10	9	10	10	9	10	10	10	10	10	10	10	10	10	10	10	10	10	10	10	10	10
	pail	0	0	0	1	0	0	1	0	0	0	0	0	0	0	0	0	0	0	0	0	0	0	0	0
44.	bucket	10	10	10	10	10	10	10	10	10	10	10	10	10	10	10	10	10	10	10	10	10	10	10	10

		upper class								middle class								lower class							
		male				female				male				female				male				female			
term	variants	< 20	20 to 40	40 to 60	60 to 80	< 20	20 to 40	40 to 60	60 to 80	< 20	20 to 40	40 to 60	60 to 80	< 20	20 to 40	40 to 60	60 to 80	< 20	20 to 40	40 to 60	60 to 80	< 20	20 to 40	40 to 60	60 to 80
45.	clean up	10	10	10	8	10	10	9	10	10	9	9	10	10	9	7	10	10	10	9	8	10	10	9	9
	tidy up	0	0	0	2	0	0	1	0	0	1	1	0	0	1	3	0	0	0	1	2	0	0	1	1
46.	spiderweb	10	10	10	10	10	10	10	10	10	10	10	10	10	10	10	10	10	10	10	10	10	10	10	10
47.	cobweb	5	6	4	7	4	5	6	5	4	6	7	4	5	6	4	6	5	4	7	5	4	8	4	7
	spiderweb	5	4	6	3	6	5	4	5	6	4	3	6	5	4	6	4	5	6	3	5	6	2	6	3
48.	cobweb	3	7	8	8	2	6	9	10	4	5	9	8	2	7	7	6	5	7	10	10	4	6	10	9
	spiderweb	7	3	2	2	8	4	1	0	6	5	1	2	8	3	3	4	5	3	0	0	6	4	0	1
49.	dust	10	10	9	10	10	8	8	10	10	10	9	10	9	10	7	10	10	9	9	10	10	10	9	10
	dustballs	0	0	0	0	0	2	0	0	0	0	0	0	1	0	0	0	0	1	0	0	0	0	0	0
	lint	0	0	1	0	0	0	2	0	0	0	1	0	0	0	3	0	0	0	1	0	0	0	1	0
50.	faucet	10	10	10	10	10	10	10	10	10	10	10	10	10	10	10	10	10	10	10	10	10	10	10	10

	term variants	upper class								middle class								lower class							
		male				female				male				female				male				female			
		< 20	20 to 40	40 to 60	60 to 80	< 20	20 to 40	40 to 60	60 to 80	< 20	20 to 40	40 to 60	60 to 80	< 20	20 to 40	40 to 60	60 to 80	< 20	20 to 40	40 to 60	60 to 80	< 20	20 to 40	40 to 60	60 to 80
51.	faucet	10	10	10	10	10	10	10	10	10	10	10	10	10	10	10	10	10	10	10	10	10	10	10	10
52.	frying pan	10	10	9	9	10	10	8	7	10	10	9	9	10	10	8	7	10	10	8	6	10	10	8	7
	skillet	0	0	1	1	0	0	2	3	0	0	1	1	0	0	2	3	0	0	2	4	0	0	2	3
53.	front room	0	0	1	2	0	0	1	1	0	0	0	2	0	0	0	1	0	0	0	0	0	0	0	0
	living room	10	10	9	8	10	10	9	9	10	10	10	8	10	10	10	9	10	10	10	10	10	10	10	10
54.	gutters	10	10	10	9	10	10	9	8	10	10	10	9	10	10	10	8	10	10	10	9	10	10	9	7
	water troughs	0	0	0	1	0	0	1	2	0	0	0	1	0	0	0	2	0	0	0	1	0	0	1	3
55.	outdoor toilet	0	3	4	0	0	2	3	0	0	0	0	0	0	0	0	0	0	0	0	0	0	0	0	0
	outhouse	10	7	6	9	10	8	7	8	10	10	9	10	10	10	9	10	10	10	10	10	10	10	10	10
	privy	0	0	0	1	0	0	0	2	0	0	1	0	0	0	1	0	0	0	0	0	0	0	0	0

	term variants	upper class								middle class								lower class							
		male				female				male				female				male				female			
		< 20	20 to 40	40 to 60	60 to 80	< 20	20 to 40	40 to 60	60 to 80	< 20	20 to 40	40 to 60	60 to 80	< 20	20 to 40	40 to 60	60 to 80	< 20	20 to 40	40 to 60	60 to 80	< 20	20 to 40	40 to 60	60 to 80
56.	front porch	10	10	10	10	10	10	10	10	10	10	10	10	10	10	10	10	9	8	9	7	9	7	7	6
	stoop	0	0	0	0	0	0	0	0	0	0	0	0	0	0	0	0	1	2	1	3	1	3	3	4
57.	fruit cellar	10	10	9	9	10	10	9	10	10	9	8	7	10	10	9	6	10	9	8	7	10	9	9	6
	root cellar	0	0	1	1	0	0	1	0	0	1	2	3	0	0	1	4	0	1	2	3	0	1	1	4
58.	fridge	4	3	1	0	5	4	1	1	3	2	0	1	1	1	0	2	1	2	2	0	1	2	2	1
	icebox	0	0	4	4	0	0	2	3	1	1	2	4	1	2	4	2	0	1	2	5	1	2	4	4
	refrigerator	6	7	5	6	5	6	7	6	6	7	8	5	8	7	6	6	9	7	6	5	8	6	4	5
59.	couch	10	10	10	10	10	9	7	9	10	10	10	10	9	8	6	9	10	10	10	10	10	9	7	8
	sofa	0	0	0	0	0	1	3	1	0	0	0	0	1	2	4	1	0	0	0	0	0	1	3	2

	term variants	upper class								middle class								lower class							
		male				female				male				female				male				female			
		< 20	20 to 40	40 to 60	60 to 80	< 20	20 to 40	40 to 60	60 to 80	< 20	20 to 40	40 to 60	60 to 80	< 20	20 to 40	40 to 60	60 to 80	< 20	20 to 40	40 to 60	60 to 80	< 20	20 to 40	40 to 60	60 to 80
60.	horse	1	0	0	0	0	0	0	0	1	2	0	0	0	0	0	0	2	2	0	0	1	0	0	0
	sawbuck	0	0	1	1	0	0	0	0	0	0	2	3	0	0	0	1	0	0	3	3	0	0	1	0
	sawhorse	9	10	9	9	10	10	10	10	9	8	8	7	10	10	10	9	8	8	7	7	10	10	9	10
61.	bag	6	7	5	6	6	7	5	4	6	7	6	5	6	7	8	9	6	7	6	5	6	9	8	7
	paper bag	4	3	5	4	4	3	5	6	4	3	4	4	4	2	2	1	4	3	4	3	4	1	2	3
	sack	0	0	0	0	0	0	0	0	0	0	0	1	0	1	0	0	0	0	0	2	0	0	0	0
62.	trash can	5	4	6	5	5	4	4	6	6	5	6	5	6	4	3	5	6	7	5	4	6	5	3	4
	waste can	5	6	4	5	5	6	6	4	4	5	4	5	4	6	7	5	4	3	5	6	4	5	7	6
63.	garbage can	0	1	2	4	0	1	1	5	0	2	1	4	0	1	3	5	0	1	1	3	0	0	2	4
	trash can	10	9	8	6	10	9	9	5	10	8	9	6	10	9	7	5	10	9	9	7	10	10	8	6

term	variants	upper class								middle class								lower class							
		male				female				male				female				male				female			
		< 20	20 to 40	40 to 60	60 to 80	< 20	20 to 40	40 to 60	60 to 80	< 20	20 to 40	40 to 60	60 to 80	< 20	20 to 40	40 to 60	60 to 80	< 20	20 to 40	40 to 60	60 to 80	< 20	20 to 40	40 to 60	60 to 80
64.	dad	10	9	9	10	8	9	10	10	10	8	10	10	9	10	10	10	10	10	9	10	9	10	10	10
	daddy	0	0	0	0	2	1	0	0	0	0	0	0	1	0	0	0	0	0	0	0	1	0	0	0
	father	0	1	1	0	0	0	0	0	0	2	0	0	0	0	0	0	0	0	1	0	0	0	0	0
65.	mom	10	9	9	10	9	8	9	10	10	9	10	10	9	9	8	10	10	9	9	10	10	10	9	10
	mommy	0	0	0	0	1	0	0	0	0	0	0	0	1	0	0	0	0	0	0	0	0	0	0	0
	mother	0	1	1	0	0	2	1	0	0	1	0	0	0	1	2	0	0	1	1	0	0	0	0	0
66.	hillbilly	0	0	0	0	0	0	0	0	0	0	0	0	0	0	0	1	0	0	0	0	0	0	0	0
	hoosier	10	10	10	10	10	10	10	10	10	10	10	10	10	10	10	9	10	10	10	10	10	10	10	10

	term variants	upper class								middle class								lower class							
		male				female				male				female				male				female			
		< 20	20 to 40	40 to 60	60 to 80	< 20	20 to 40	40 to 60	60 to 80	< 20	20 to 40	40 to 60	60 to 80	< 20	20 to 40	40 to 60	60 to 80	< 20	20 to 40	40 to 60	60 to 80	< 20	20 to 40	40 to 60	60 to 80
67.	black	10	6	4	4	10	7	5	6	10	6	5	4	10	7	6	4	10	4	6	5	10	7	6	5
	colored	0	2	1	1	0	0	2	1	0	1	0	0	0	0	2	2	0	1	1	2	0	1	1	2
	coon	0	0	1	0	0	1	0	0	0	0	1	0	0	0	0	1	0	1	0	0	0	0	1	0
	negro	0	2	2	3	0	1	1	2	0	1	1	4	0	1	0	1	0	2	1	1	0	1	1	2
	nigger	0	0	0	0	0	0	0	0	0	0	0	1	0	0	0	1	0	0	0	2	0	0	0	1
	spook	0	0	2	2	0	1	2	1	0	2	3	1	0	2	2	1	0	2	2	0	0	1	1	0
68.	coon	0	0	0	0	0	0	0	0	0	0	0	1	0	0	0	0	0	0	1	1	0	0	0	0
	hillbilly	0	0	0	0	0	0	0	0	0	0	0	1	0	0	0	0	0	0	0	0	0	0	0	0
	hoosier	6	3	6	5	5	6	6	6	3	2	6	4	4	6	4	7	3	3	6	6	5	6	5	6
	nigger	3	7	4	4	5	4	4	4	6	8	3	4	6	4	6	3	6	5	3	3	5	3	4	4
	spook	1	0	0	1	0	0	0	0	1	0	1	0	0	0	0	0	1	2	0	0	0	1	1	0

	term variants	upper class								middle class								lower class							
		male				female				male				female				male				female			
		< 20	20 to 40	40 to 60	60 to 80	< 20	20 to 40	40 to 60	60 to 80	< 20	20 to 40	40 to 60	60 to 80	< 20	20 to 40	40 to 60	60 to 80	< 20	20 to 40	40 to 60	60 to 80	< 20	20 to 40	40 to 60	60 to 80
69.	cop	4	5	6	5	4	5	2	3	6	6	6	5	6	7	5	4	7	6	6	8	6	8	4	4
	fuzz	0	0	0	0	0	0	0	0	0	1	0	0	0	0	0	0	0	0	0	0	0	0	0	0
	pig	0	0	0	0	0	0	0	0	0	0	0	0	0	0	0	0	1	1	0	0	1	0	0	0
	policeman	6	5	4	5	6	5	8	7	4	3	4	5	4	3	5	6	2	3	4	2	3	2	6	6
70.	relations	0	0	0	1	0	0	0	0	0	0	0	0	0	0	0	0	0	0	0	0	0	0	0	0
	relatives	10	10	10	9	10	10	10	10	10	10	10	10	10	10	10	10	10	10	10	10	10	10	10	10
71.	guys	6	5	5	4	6	6	7	5	4	5	6	7	5	4	6	4	6	5	4	7	6	4	5	5
	you guys	4	5	4	6	4	4	3	5	6	5	4	3	5	6	4	6	4	5	5	3	4	6	5	5
	youse guys	0	0	1	0	0	0	0	0	0	0	0	0	0	0	0	0	0	0	1	0	0	0	0	0
72.	firehouse	6	7	6	5	6	5	4	6	7	6	4	5	5	6	5	6	4	5	5	5	6	4	6	5
	firestation	4	3	4	5	4	5	6	4	3	4	6	5	5	4	5	4	6	5	5	5	4	6	4	5

	term variants	upper class								middle class								lower class							
		male				female				male				female				male				female			
		< 20	20 to 40	40 to 60	60 to 80	< 20	20 to 40	40 to 60	60 to 80	< 20	20 to 40	40 to 60	60 to 80	< 20	20 to 40	40 to 60	60 to 80	< 20	20 to 40	40 to 60	60 to 80	< 20	20 to 40	40 to 60	60 to 80
73.	fire hydrant	3	2	7	6	1	2	6	5	4	2	5	4	2	1	9	7	2	1	7	6	4	2	8	7
	fireplug	1	1	2	2	2	1	2	3	0	1	3	5	1	1	0	2	2	3	0	2	1	1	1	1
	hydrant	6	7	1	2	7	7	2	2	6	7	2	1	7	8	1	1	6	6	3	2	5	7	1	2
74.	seesaw	10	10	9	7	10	10	8	8	10	10	9	9	10	10	7	6	10	9	8	8	10	10	7	9
	teeter totter	0	0	1	3	0	0	2	2	0	0	1	1	0	0	3	4	0	1	2	2	0	0	3	1
75.	eighteen-whler.	9	3	1	1	8	1	0	0	10	1	1	1	8	0	2	1	9	0	0	1	9	0	0	0
	MAC truck	0	2	3	0	1	3	4	1	0	4	3	0	1	4	3	0	1	4	5	1	1	6	5	0
	semi	1	4	5	1	1	6	6	0	0	4	5	0	1	5	5	1	0	5	5	2	0	4	4	2
	tractor-trailer	0	1	1	8	0	0	0	9	0	1	1	9	0	1	0	8	0	1	0	6	0	0	1	8

term	variants	upper class								middle class								lower class							
		male				female				male				female				male				female			
		< 20	20 to 40	40 to 60	60 to 80	< 20	20 to 40	40 to 60	60 to 80	< 20	20 to 40	40 to 60	60 to 80	< 20	20 to 40	40 to 60	60 to 80	< 20	20 to 40	40 to 60	60 to 80	< 20	20 to 40	40 to 60	60 to 80
76.	dock	8	7	9	10	8	7	8	8	9	8	6	8	7	8	9	7	8	10	9	8	7	7	6	6
	pier	2	3	1	0	2	3	2	1	1	2	4	2	3	2	1	2	2	0	1	1	3	3	4	4
	wharf	0	0	0	0	0	0	0	1	0	0	0	0	0	0	0	1	0	0	0	1	0	0	0	0
77.	belly bumper	2	3	1	0	2	3	4	1	1	2	2	2	3	2	1	0	2	1	1	0	0	2	3	1
	belly buster	8	7	9	10	8	7	6	7	9	8	8	8	7	8	9	10	8	9	9	10	10	8	7	8
78.	belly buster	0	2	3	4	0	1	1	2	0	2	4	3	0	3	2	1	4	4	2	1	3	2	2	2
	belly flop	10	8	7	6	10	9	9	7	10	8	6	7	10	7	8	9	6	6	8	9	7	8	8	7
79.	belch	4	3	4	5	2	3	4	3	6	7	7	8	5	6	7	8	9	10	9	10	9	8	7	9
	burp	6	7	6	5	8	7	6	7	4	3	3	2	5	4	3	2	1	0	1	0	1	2	3	1
80.	catty-corner	10	10	10	10	10	10	10	10	10	10	10	10	10	10	10	10	10	10	10	8	10	10	10	10
	kitty-corner	0	0	0	0	0	0	0	0	0	0	0	0	0	0	0	0	0	0	0	2	0	0	0	0

	term variants	upper class								middle class								lower class							
		male				female				male				female				male				female			
		< 20	20 to 40	40 to 60	60 to 80	< 20	20 to 40	40 to 60	60 to 80	< 20	20 to 40	40 to 60	60 to 80	< 20	20 to 40	40 to 60	60 to 80	< 20	20 to 40	40 to 60	60 to 80	< 20	20 to 40	40 to 60	60 to 80
81.	escort	0	0	0	0	0	0	0	8	0	0	0	0	0	0	0	0	0	0	0	0	0	0	0	0
	take	10	10	10	10	10	10	10	2	10	10	10	10	10	10	10	10	10	10	10	10	10	10	10	10
82.	favors	0	0	0	0	0	0	0	0	0	0	1	0	0	0	2	0	0	0	2	2	0	0	1	2
	looks like	8	7	6	5	6	7	6	6	6	6	7	6	5	5	7	6	4	3	3	6	5	3	5	5
	resembles	2	3	4	5	4	3	4	4	2	1	2	1	3	2	1	2	3	2	3	2	1	2	2	3
	takes after	0	0	0	0	0	0	0	0	2	3	0	3	2	3	0	2	3	5	2	2	4	5	2	0
83.	crawl	10	10	10	10	10	10	10	10	10	10	10	10	10	10	10	10	10	10	10	10	10	10	10	10
84.	look after	0	0	0	0	0	0	0	0	0	0	0	0	0	0	0	0	0	0	0	2	0	0	3	2
	take care of	10	10	10	10	10	10	10	10	10	10	10	10	10	10	10	10	10	10	10	8	10	10	7	8
85.	brought up	0	0	0	0	0	0	0	0	0	0	0	0	0	0	0	0	0	0	2	1	0	0	3	2
	raised	10	10	10	10	10	10	10	10	10	10	10	10	10	10	10	10	10	10	8	9	10	10	7	8

term	variants	upper class								middle class								lower class							
		male				female				male				female				male				female			
		< 20	20 to 40	40 to 60	60 to 80	< 20	20 to 40	40 to 60	60 to 80	< 20	20 to 40	40 to 60	60 to 80	< 20	20 to 40	40 to 60	60 to 80	< 20	20 to 40	40 to 60	60 to 80	< 20	20 to 40	40 to 60	60 to 80
86.	be truant	0	0	2	4	0	1	5	4	0	0	0	0	0	2	2	2	0	0	0	0	0	1	0	0
	play hookey	0	0	2	4	0	1	5	4	0	0	0	0	0	2	2	2	0	0	0	0	0	1	0	0
	skip	10	2	1	0	10	2	0	0	10	1	1	1	10	1	1	0	10	0	1	1	10	1	1	0
	skip class	0	1	1	0	0	1	0	0	0	2	1	0	0	1	0	0	0	2	0	0	0	1	1	0
	skip school	0	3	0	1	0	2	1	1	0	4	1	1	0	2	0	1	0	3	1	1	0	3	0	1
87.	long way	3	2	2	1	2	2	3	4	5	2	3	4	3	2	1	0	2	1	3	2	1	2	2	3
	long ways	7	8	8	9	8	8	7	6	5	8	7	6	7	8	9	10	8	9	7	8	9	8	8	7
88.	slick	4	3	4	5	3	2	3	4	4	5	6	4	5	5	4	4	6	5	6	7	7	6	7	7
	slippery	6	7	6	5	7	8	7	6	6	5	4	6	5	5	6	6	4	5	4	3	3	4	3	3
89.	binoculars	10	9	2	3	10	8	2	2	10	9	3	4	10	9	3	2	9	9	2	0	10	10	1	1
	field glasses	0	1	8	7	0	2	8	8	0	1	7	6	0	1	7	8	1	1	8	10	0	0	9	9

	term variants	upper class								middle class								lower class							
		male				female				male				female				male				female			
		< 20	20 to 40	40 to 60	60 to 80	< 20	20 to 40	40 to 60	60 to 80	< 20	20 to 40	40 to 60	60 to 80	< 20	20 to 40	40 to 60	60 to 80	< 20	20 to 40	40 to 60	60 to 80	< 20	20 to 40	40 to 60	60 to 80
90.	casket	4	3	4	5	3	2	3	3	4	5	6	5	4	4	5	5	7	6	7	8	6	8	8	7
	coffin	6	7	6	5	7	8	7	7	6	5	4	5	6	6	5	5	3	4	3	2	4	2	2	3
91.	grease job	4	3	4	4	3	3	2	3	5	6	6	7	5	6	7	8	5	5	5	7	8	8	7	7
	greased	6	7	6	6	7	7	8	7	5	4	4	3	5	4	3	2	5	4	3	2	2	1	2	3
	lube job	0	0	0	0	0	0	0	0	0	0	0	0	0	0	0	0	0	1	2	1	0	1	1	0
92.	harmonica	10	10	10	9	10	10	10	8	10	10	10	8	10	10	10	7	10	10	9	7	10	10	10	8
	mouth harp	0	0	0	1	0	0	0	2	0	0	0	2	0	0	0	3	0	0	1	3	0	0	0	2
93.	baby buggy	10	10	7	6	10	10	6	6	10	10	8	8	10	10	10	9	10	10	9	9	10	10	10	7
	baby carriage	0	0	1	2	0	0	2	1	0	0	2	0	0	0	0	0	0	0	1	0	0	0	0	2
	carriage	0	0	2	2	0	0	2	3	0	0	0	2	0	0	0	1	0	0	1	1	0	0	0	1

	term variants	upper class								middle class								lower class							
		male				female				male				female				male				female			
		< 20	20 to 40	40 to 60	60 to 80	< 20	20 to 40	40 to 60	60 to 80	< 20	20 to 40	40 to 60	60 to 80	< 20	20 to 40	40 to 60	60 to 80	< 20	20 to 40	40 to 60	60 to 80	< 20	20 to 40	40 to 60	60 to 80
94.	bathing suit	0	0	0	0	0	0	4	6	0	0	0	0	0	0	6	4	0	0	0	0	0	0	0	0
	swim suit	10	7	6	8	10	8	5	4	10	7	6	8	10	8	4	4	10	9	9	7	9	7	5	6
	swim trunks	0	3	4	2	0	2	1	0	0	3	4	2	0	2	0	2	0	1	1	3	1	3	5	4
95.	sled	8	7	8	7	6	7	8	9	10	9	9	8	7	7	6	5	6	7	8	7	6	5	5	6
	sleigh	2	3	2	3	4	3	2	1	0	1	1	2	3	3	4	5	4	3	2	3	4	5	5	4
96.	ghost	10	10	10	10	10	10	10	10	10	10	10	10	10	10	10	10	10	10	10	10	9	10	10	10
	spook	0	0	0	0	0	0	0	0	0	0	0	0	0	0	0	0	0	0	0	0	1	0	0	0

Lexical Index

Below is an index of all the lexical items recorded in the survey. Numbers correspond to the semantic categories given earlier.

6. CONCLUSIONS

Thus far I have given an extensive empirical account of the phonology, morphology, syntax, and lexicon of St. Louis; now I would like to return to the questions posed at the end of Chapter 1 and offer answers based on my data.

1. Can significant patterns in the language of St. Louis be discovered when it is viewed as a function of such independent variables as the age, gender, and socioeconomic class of its users?

In approaching an answer to this question, it becomes useful to regroup the data from Chapters 3, 4, and 5 into the relevant demographic categories; that is, rather than examine the speech of, for example, lower class females between the ages of 40 and 60, some of the demographic boundaries used previously must be collapsed and new ones created to examine the speech of the entire lower class, all females, all informants aged 40 to 60, and so on. The following pages contain all of the data thus regrouped, with raw scores converted to percentages for the sake of clarity. In the section on phonology, "NA" indicates that the data were not available for the demographic group in question. In the sections on morphology/syntax and lexicon, the terms have again been numbered to correspond with the numerical system used in Chapters 4 and 5.

Phonology

sound in question	socioeconomic class of informants			contextual formality			gender of informants		age of informants						
	upper	middle	lower	informal	midformal	formal	male	female	< 30	< 40	30-60	40-60	< 60	> 60	ALL
post-vocalic [r]	100	100	100	100	100	100	100	100	100	100	100	100	100	100	100
[w] (wheel, whip, etc.)	99	100	100	100	100	99	100	100	100	100	100	100	100	100	100
[hw] (wheel, whip, etc.)	1	0	0	0	0	1	0	0	0	0	0	0	0	0	0
[j] (humor)	50	54	53	56	48	53	NA	NA	NA	NA	NA	NA	NA	NA	52
[hj] (humor)	50	46	47	44	52	47	NA	NA	NA	NA	NA	NA	NA	NA	48
affricate in garage	58	55	55	57	56	55	NA	NA	NA	NA	NA	NA	NA	NA	56
fricative in garage	42	45	45	43	44	45	NA	NA	NA	NA	NA	NA	NA	NA	44
voiced inter-dental in with, without	55	55	50	56	52	49	NA	NA	NA	NA	NA	NA	NA	NA	53

sound in question	socioeconomic class of informants			contextual formality			gender of informants		age of informants						ALL
	upper	middle	lower	informal	midformal	formal	male	female	< 30	< 40	30-60	40-60	< 60	> 60	
voiceless interdental in with, without	45	45	50	44	48	51	NA	NA	NA	NA	NA	NA	NA	NA	47
intrusive [r]	63	73	83	91	75	53	NA	NA	NA	NA	NA	NA	NA	NA	73
initial [z] (sink, etc.)	2	15	27	25	15	7	NA	NA	NA	NA	NA	NA	13	20	16
initial [s] (sink, etc.)	98	85	73	25	85	83	NA	NA	NA	NA	NA	NA	87	80	84
medial [z] (greasy, etc.)	11	42	64	53	44	31	NA	NA	NA	NA	NA	NA	39	47	43
medial [s] (greasy, etc.)	89	58	36	47	56	69	NA	NA	NA	NA	NA	NA	NA	NA	57
[j] (yeast)	78	64	57	59	65	76	NA	NA	NA	98	NA	85	NA	17	67
no [j] (yeast)	22	36	43	41	35	24	NA	NA	NA	2	NA	15	NA	83	33
[l] (palm)	79	31	0	27	39	51	NA	NA	NA	NA	NA	NA	NA	NA	39

sound in question	socioeconomic class of informants			contextual formality			gender of informants		age of informants						
	upper	middle	lower	informal	midformal	formal	male	female	< 30	< 40	30- 60	40- 60	< 60	> 60	ALL
no [l] (palm)	21	69	100	73	61	49	NA	NA	NA	NA	NA	NA	NA	NA	61
medial [r] deleted in quarter	42	67	97	79	68	60	NA	NA	NA	NA	NA	NA	NA	NA	69
medial [r] retained in quarter	58	33	3	21	32	40	NA	NA	NA	NA	NA	NA	NA	NA	31
Mrs. as two syllables	70	50	38	41	54	67	56	50	NA	41	NA	55	NA	63	53
Mrs. as one syllable	30	50	62	59	46	33	44	50	NA	59	NA	45	NA	37	47
low front vowel (bath, etc.)	98	99	100	100	99	98	NA	NA	NA	NA	NA	NA	NA	NA	99
low central vowel (bath, etc.)	2	1	0	0	1	2	NA	NA	NA	NA	NA	NA	NA	NA	1

sound in question	socioeconomic class of informants			contextual formality			gender of informants		age of informants						
	upper	middle	lower	informal	midformal	formal	male	female	< 30	< 40	30-60	40-60	< 60	> 60	ALL
mid front lax vowel (pen, penny)	100	100	98	98	99	100	NA	NA	NA	NA	NA	NA	NA	NA	99
high front lax vowel (pen, penny)	0	0	2	2	1	0	NA	NA	NA	NA	NA	NA	NA	NA	1
low back vowel (log, fog, on)	100	100	100	100	100	100	100	100	100	100	100	100	100	100	100
low back vowel (foreign, orange)	96	100	100	99	98	98	NA	NA	NA	NA	NA	NA	NA	NA	99
low central vowel (foreign, orange)	4	0	0	1	2	2	NA	NA	NA	NA	NA	NA	NA	NA	1
low back vowel (water)	100	100	100	100	100	100	100	100	100	100	100	100	100	100	100

sound in question	socioeconomic class of informants			contextual formality			gender of informants		age of informants						
	upper	middle	lower	informal	midformal	formal	male	female	< 30	< 40	30-60	40-60	< 60	> 60	ALL
mid front lax vowel (Mary, marry, merry)	100	100	100	100	100	100	100	100	100	100	100	100	100	100	100
[i] (either, neither)	98	100	100	100	99	99	NA	NA	NA	NA	NA	NA	NA	NA	99
diphthong (either, neither)	2	0	0	0	1	1	NA	NA	NA	NA	NA	NA	NA	NA	1
high front lax vowel (stomach)	100	100	99	99	100	100	100	100	100	100	100	100	100	100	100
mid-central vowel (stomach)	0	0	1	1	0	0	0	0	0	0	0	0	0	0	0
low central to high front lax diphthong (bite, etc.)	100	100	100	100	100	100	100	100	100	100	100	100	100	100	100

sound in question	socioeconomic class of informants			contextual formality			gender of informants		age of informants						
	upper	middle	lower	informal	midformal	formal	male	female	< 30	< 40	30- 60	40- 60	< 60	> 60	ALL
low central to high back lax diphthong (house, etc.)	100	100	100	100	100	100	100	100	100	100	100	100	100	100	100
[u] (route)	57	56	50	52	56	55	NA	NA	NA	NA	NA	NA	NA	NA	55
high back lax vowel (route)	43	44	50	48	44	45	NA	NA	NA	NA	NA	NA	NA	NA	45
[u] (roof)	70	74	69	69	73	71	NA	NA	NA	NA	NA	NA	NA	NA	71
high back lax vowel (roof)	30	26	31	31	27	29	NA	NA	NA	NA	NA	NA	NA	NA	29
low back vowel (hearth)	60	68	66	64	65	65	NA	NA	NA	NA	NA	NA	NA	NA	65
mid-central vowel (hearth)	40	32	34	36	35	35	NA	NA	NA	NA	NA	NA	NA	NA	35
[i] (depot)	71	64	71	71	64	71	NA	NA	NA	NA	NA	NA	NA	NA	68

sound in question	socioeconomic class of informants			contextual formality			gender of informants		age of informants						
	upper	middle	lower	informal	midformal	formal	male	female	< 30	< 40	30-60	40-60	< 60	> 60	ALL
mid front lax vowel (depot)	29	36	29	29	36	29	NA	NA	NA	NA	NA	NA	NA	NA	32
[e] (patronize)	67	71	68	67	70	69	NA	NA	NA	NA	NA	NA	NA	NA	69
low front vowel (patronize)	33	29	32	33	30	31	NA	NA	NA	NA	NA	NA	NA	NA	31
mid-central vowel (because)	54	51	50	52	50	52	NA	NA	NA	NA	NA	NA	NA	NA	52
low back vowel (because)	46	49	50	48	50	48	NA	NA	NA	NA	NA	NA	NA	NA	48
pre-r /o/ = [o]	79	56	28	31	56	73	NA	NA	NA	NA	NA	NA	NA	NA	53
pre-r /o/ = low back vowel	21	44	72	69	44	27	NA	NA	NA	NA	NA	NA	NA	NA	47
pre-r /o/ (with with constraints) = low back vowel	0	0	0	0	0	0	0	0	0	0	0	0	0	0	0

sound in question	socioeconomic class of informants			contextual formality			gender of informants		age of informants						
	upper	middle	lower	informal	midformal	formal	male	female	< 30	< 40	30- 60	40- 60	< 60	> 60	ALL
[a] (pajamas, pecan, plaza)	82	72	4	39	55	63	NA	NA	62	NA	53	NA	NA	43	52
low front vowel (pajamas, pecan, plaza)	18	28	96	61	45	37	NA	NA	38	NA	47	NA	NA	57	48
[e] (egg(s))	12	27	39	33	25	19	NA	NA	NA	NA	NA	NA	2	50	26
mid front lax vowel (egg(s))	88	73	61	67	75	81	NA	NA	NA	NA	NA	NA	98	50	74
[u] (due, etc.)	58	89	100	91	83	73	NA	NA	NA	NA	NA	NA	NA	NA	83
[ju] (due, etc.)	42	11	0	9	17	27	NA	NA	NA	NA	NA	NA	NA	NA	17
[u] (coupon)	50	64	75	73	62	54	NA	NA	NA	NA	NA	NA	NA	NA	63
[ju] (coupon)	50	36	25	27	38	46	NA	NA	NA	NA	NA	NA	NA	NA	37
mid front lax vowel (catch)	76	80	100	88	92	88	NA	NA	76	NA	100	100	NA	100	89

sound in question	socioeconomic class of informants			contextual formality			gender of informants		age of informants						
	upper	middle	lower	informal	midformal	formal	male	female	< 30	< 40	30- 60	40- 60	< 60	> 60	ALL
low front vowel (catch)	24	20	0	12	8	12	NA	NA	24	NA	0	0	NA	0	11
[i] (creek)	100	89	80	92	89	89	NA	NA	100	NA	80	80	NA	80	90
high front lax vowel (creek)	0	11	20	8	11	11	NA	NA	0	NA	20	20	NA	20	10
mid front lax vowel (bury)	53	69	90	85	75	65	NA	NA	NA	NA	NA	NA	NA	NA	74
mid-central vowel (bury)	47	31	10	15	25	35	NA	NA	NA	NA	NA	NA	NA	NA	26
low back vowel (sausage)	99	98	86	92	95	96	NA	NA	100	100	100	100	NA	82	94
low central vowel (sausage)	1	2	14	8	5	4	NA	NA	0	0	0	0	NA	18	6
mid-central vowel (sundae)	79	86	90	95	87	71	NA	NA	NA	NA	NA	NA	NA	NA	85
[i] (sundae)	12	12	10	3	11	21	NA	NA	NA	NA	NA	NA	NA	NA	11

sound in question	socioeconomic class of informants			contextual formality			gender of informants		age of informants						
	upper	middle	lower	informal	midformal	formal	male	female	< 30	< 40	30-60	40-60	< 60	> 60	ALL
[e] (sundae)	10	2	0	0	3	8	NA	NA	NA	NA	NA	NA	NA	NA	4
mid-central vowel (Missouri + consonant)	6	15	34	29	18	7	NA	NA	14	NA	20	20	NA	20	18
[i] (Missouri + consonant)	94	85	66	71	82	93	NA	NA	86	NA	80	80	NA	80	82
mid-central vowel (Missouri + vowel)	3	9	26	21	12	4	NA	NA	7	NA	16	16	NA	NA	12
[i] (Missouri + consonant)	97	91	74	79	88	96	NA	NA	93	NA	84	84	NA	NA	88
mid-central vowel (Missouri + ##)	4	9	28	26	16	1	NA	NA	10	NA	20	20	NA	20	15
[i] (Missouri + ##)	96	91	72	74	84	99	NA	NA	90	NA	80	80	NA	80	85

sound in question	socioeconomic class of informants			contextual formality			gender of informants		age of informants						
	upper	middle	lower	informal	midformal	formal	male	female	< 30	< 40	30-60	40-60	< 60	> 60	ALL
mid-central vowel (potato, tomato + consonant)	33	57	100	75	60	51	NA	NA	NA	NA	NA	NA	NA	NA	62
[o] (potato, tomato + consonant)	67	43	0	25	40	49	NA	NA	NA	NA	NA	NA	NA	NA	62
mid-central vowel (potato, tomato + vowel)	20	37	59	51	39	27	NA	NA	NA	NA	NA	NA	NA	NA	39
[o] (potato, tomato + vowel)	80	63	41	49	61	73	NA	NA	NA	NA	NA	NA	NA	NA	61
mid-central vowel (potato, tomato + ##)	23	50	81	65	53	36	NA	NA	NA	NA	NA	NA	NA	NA	50
[o] (potato, tomato + ##)	77	50	19	35	47	64	NA	NA	NA	NA	NA	NA	NA	NA	50

term	variants	socioeconomic class of informants			gender of informants		age of informants				
		upper	middle	lower	male	female	< 20	20-40	40-60	> 60	ALL
1.	bit	5	21	86	46	29	28	35	40	47	38
	bitten	95	79	14	54	71	72	65	60	53	62
2.	blew	100	100	91	98	97	100	100	100	88	97
	blowed	0	0	1	1	0	0	0	0	2	0
	blown	0	0	8	1	3	0	0	0	10	3
3.	broke	0	23	54	31	20	12	18	28	43	25
	broken	100	77	46	69	80	88	82	72	57	75
4.	burst	100	64	21	60	63	80	60	57	50	25
	bursted	0	36	79	40	37	20	40	43	50	75
5.	bought	100	100	99	99	100	100	100	100	98	100
	boughten	0	0	1	1	0	0	0	0	2	0

term	variants	socioeconomic class of informants			gender of informants		age of informants				ALL
		upper	middle	lower	male	female	< 20	20-40	40-60	> 60	
6.	caught	100	100	100	100	100	100	100	100	100	100
7.	climbed	100	100	98	99	99	100	100	100	97	99
	clumb	0	0	2	1	1	0	0	0	3	1
8.	came	99	54	26	8	61	65	62	60	52	60
	come	1	46	74	92	39	35	38	40	48	40
9.	dived	4	16	28	19	13	8	12	17	27	16
	dove	96	84	72	81	87	92	88	83	73	84
10.	did	100	99	63	82	89	95	92	85	77	85
	done	0	1	37	18	11	5	8	15	23	15
11.	dragged	99	84	59	78	83	90	82	75	75	80
	drug	1	16	41	22	17	10	18	25	25	20

term	variants	socioeconomic class of informants			gender of informants		age of informants				
		upper	middle	lower	male	female	< 20	20-40	40-60	> 60	ALL
12.	drawn	0	1	0	1	0	0	0	2	0	0
	drew	100	99	100	99	100	100	100	98	100	100
13.	dreamed	8	16	35	26	13	15	20	20	23	39
	dreamt	92	84	65	74	87	85	80	80	77	61
14.	drank	100	100	94	98	98	100	100	100	92	98
	drunk	0	0	6	2	2	0	0	0	8	2
15.	drank	0	1	20	7	8	5	7	5	8	7
	drunk	100	99	80	83	82	95	83	95	92	93
16.	drove	100	100	100	100	100	100	100	100	100	100
17.	driven	100	100	71	90	91	98	95	85	83	90
	drove	0	0	29	10	9	2	5	15	17	10

		socioeconomic class of informants			gender of informants		age of informants				
term	variants	upper	middle	lower	male	female	< 20	20-40	40-60	> 60	ALL
18.	drownded	1	5	41	18	13	12	10	17	25	16
	drowned	99	95	59	82	87	88	90	83	75	84
19.	ate	100	100	100	100	100	100	100	100	100	100
20.	ate	0	0	9	4	2	0	0	5	7	3
	eaten	100	100	91	96	98	100	100	100	100	100
21.	fought	100	100	100	100	100	100	100	100	100	100
22.	fit	99	92	75	85	92	90	82	82	88	89
	fitted	1	8	25	15	18	10	18	18	12	11
23.	gave	100	93	73	88	90	93	95	82	83	89
	give	0	7	27	12	10	7	5	18	17	11
24.	grew	100	100	100	100	100	100	100	100	100	100

		socioeconomic class of informants			gender of informants		age of informants				
term	variants	upper	middle	lower	male	female	< 20	20-40	40-60	> 60	ALL
25.	grew	0	0	15	4	6	3	2	8	7	5
	grown	100	100	85	96	94	97	98	92	93	95
26.	hanged	100	99	84	93	96	95	98	93	90	94
	hung	0	1	16	7	4	5	2	7	10	6
27.	heard	100	100	100	100	100	100	100	100	100	100
28.	heat	0	0	4	2	1	0	0	0	5	1
	heated	100	100	96	98	99	100	100	100	95	99
29.	helped	100	100	100	100	100	100	100	100	100	100
30.	helped	100	100	100	100	100	100	100	100	100	100
31.	kneeled	0	1	19	7	7	2	3	8	13	7
	knelt	100	99	81	93	93	98	97	92	87	93

		socioeconomic class of informants			gender of informants		age of informants				
term	variants	upper	middle	lower	male	female	< 20	20-40	40-60	> 60	ALL
32.	knit	0	0	10	0	7	0	2	7	5	3
	knitted	100	100	90	100	93	100	98	93	95	97
33.	knew	100	90	79	87	92	97	95	85	82	94
	knowed	0	0	1	0	1	0	0	0	1	0
	known	0	10	20	13	7	3	5	15	17	6
34.	lended	0	10	18	10	8	5	13	10	8	9
	lent	55	45	73	57	61	95	58	57	58	58
	loaned	45	45	10	33	31	0	29	33	34	33
35.	lay	48	74	89	70	70	62	67	72	80	70
	lie	52	26	11	30	30	38	33	28	20	30
36.	laid	79	99	100	94	91	90	92	93	95	98
	lay	21	1	0	6	9	10	8	7	5	2

term	variants	socioeconomic class of informants			gender of informants		age of informants				ALL
		upper	middle	lower	male	female	< 20	20-40	40-60	> 60	
37.	pleaded	56	69	93	72	73	83	80	67	60	73
	pled	44	31	7	28	27	17	20	33	40	27
38.	rid	0	25	36	22	19	4	15	28	32	20
	ridden	100	65	46	67	74	80	80	65	62	70
	rode	0	10	18	11	7	16	5	7	6	10
39.	rang	100	86	55	77	84	90	83	77	72	80
	rung	0	14	45	23	16	10	17	23	28	20
40.	arose	0	6	11	7	5	0	0	8	15	6
	rose	100	94	89	93	95	100	100	92	85	94
41.	ran	99	75	59	70	85	83	78	78	70	78
	run	1	25	41	30	15	17	22	22	30	22

term	variants	socioeconomic class of informants			gender of informants		age of informants				ALL
		upper	middle	lower	male	female	< 20	20-40	40-60	> 60	
42.	saw	100	87	74	81	93	92	87	87	83	87
	seen	0	13	26	19	7	8	13	13	17	13
43.	set	49	45	50	52	44	47	45	52	48	48
	sit	51	55	50	48	56	53	55	48	52	52
44.	sat	29	53	49	48	38	38	43	38	53	43
	set	71	47	51	52	62	62	57	62	47	57
45.	sewed	5	15	61	29	25	25	25	28	30	27
	sewn	95	85	39	71	75	75	75	72	70	73
46.	shrank	99	63	83	83	80	85	82	78	80	81
	shrunk	1	37	17	17	20	15	18	22	20	19
47.	set	0	0	10	4	3	0	0	5	8	3
	sit	100	100	90	96	97	100	100	95	92	97

term	variants	socioeconomic class of informants			gender of informants		age of informants				ALL
		upper	middle	lower	male	female	< 20	20-40	40-60	> 60	
48.	sat	100	100	99	99	99	100	100	100	95	100
	set	0	0	1	1	1	0	0	0	5	0
49.	sneaked	0	20	19	13	13	3	8	18	22	15
	snuck	100	80	81	87	87	97	92	82	78	85
50.	spoiled	100	100	88	61	64	100	100	93	90	96
	spoilt	0	0	12	39	36	0	0	7	10	4
51.	stole	100	100	97	98	100	100	100	100	97	99
	stoled	0	0	3	2	0	0	0	0	3	1
52.	sweat	24	3	0	11	7	10	8	7	10	9
	sweated	76	97	100	89	93	90	92	93	90	91
53.	swelled	89	79	51	65	81	82	80	68	62	73
	swoll	11	21	49	35	19	18	20	32	38	27

term	variants	socioeconomic class of informants			gender of informants		age of informants				ALL
		upper	middle	lower	male	female	< 20	20-40	40-60	> 60	
54.	swelled	13	20	48	32	22	23	25	27	32	27
	swollen	87	80	52	68	78	77	75	73	68	73
55.	swam	100	100	90	95	98	100	100	100	87	97
	swum	0	0	10	5	2	0	0	0	13	3
56.	took	100	100	100	100	100	100	100	100	100	100
57.	taken	100	90	75	88	89	92	90	88	83	88
	took	0	10	25	12	11	8	10	12	17	12
58.	taught	100	100	100	100	100	100	100	100	100	100
59.	tore	97	74	43	67	76	80	77	70	58	71
	torn	3	26	57	33	24	20	23	30	42	29
60.	threw	100	100	83	93	95	97	95	92	90	94
	throwed	0	0	17	7	5	3	5	8	10	6

		socioeconomic class of informants			gender of informants		age of informants				
term	variants	upper	middle	lower	male	female	< 20	20-40	40-60	> 60	ALL
61.	waked	0	0	1	0	1	0	0	0	1	0
	woke	100	100	99	100	99	100	100	100	99	100
62.	wore	3	22	38	18	22	13	17	27	33	21
	worn	97	78	62	82	78	87	83	73	67	79
63.	written	100	100	100	100	100	100	100	100	100	100
64.	am	100	100	100	100	100	100	100	100	100	100
65.	are	100	100	100	100	100	100	100	100	100	100
66.	costs	100	100	100	100	100	100	100	100	100	100
67.	does	100	100	100	100	100	100	100	100	100	100
68.	have	100	100	100	100	100	100	100	100	100	100
69.	I been	6	42	66	43	38	33	37	43	47	38
	I've been	94	58	34	57	62	67	63	57	53	62
70.	makes	100	100	100	100	100	100	100	100	100	100

		socioeconomic class of informants			gender of informants		age of informants				
term	variants	upper	middle	lower	male	female	< 20	20-40	40-60	> 60	ALL
71.	rinses	100	100	100	100	100	100	100	100	100	100
72.	say	100	100	61	88	87	95	85	83	57	87
	says	0	0	39	12	13	5	15	17	43	13
73.	work	100	100	100	100	100	100	100	100	100	100
74.	work	100	100	100	100	100	100	100	100	100	100
75.	are	100	100	100	100	100	100	100	100	100	100
76.	're	60	50	34	47	49	52	45	50	45	48
	's	40	50	66	53	51	48	55	50	55	52
77.	are	100	100	100	100	100	100	100	100	100	100
78.	're	100	75	43	70	75	82	75	70	63	73
	's	0	25	57	30	25	18	25	30	37	27

term	variants	socioeconomic class of informants			gender of informants		age of informants				ALL
		upper	middle	lower	male	female	< 20	20-40	40-60	> 60	
79.	was	0	14	33	17	14	13	17	18	13	31
	were	100	86	67	83	86	87	83	82	87	69
80.	was	100	100	100	100	100	100	100	100	100	100
81.	say	100	100	70	92	88	97	97	88	80	90
	says	0	0	30	18	12	3	3	12	20	10
82.	think	100	100	100	100	100	100	100	100	100	100
83.	I ain't	4	44	85	44	44	35	25	45	55	44
	I'm not	96	56	15	56	56	65	75	55	45	56
84.	ain't I	6	48	84	52	40	38	43	48	53	46
	am I not	50	26	9	27	30	38	30	23	22	28
	aren't I	44	26	7	21	30	24	27	29	25	26

term	variants	socioeconomic class of informants			gender of informants		age of informants				
		upper	middle	lower	male	female	< 20	20- 40	40- 60	> 60	ALL
85.	wan't he	0	0	8	3	3	0	0	1	8	3
	warn't he	0	0	1	1	0	0	0	0	1	0
	wasn't he	100	100	91	96	97	100	100	99	91	97
86.	dare not	100	85	81	88	90	99	95	83	78	89
	daren't	0	15	14	10	9	1	5	13	18	10
	dasn't	0	0	5	2	1	0	0	4	4	1
87.	ain't	0	23	68	32	30	23	28	33	35	30
	haven't	100	77	32	68	70	77	72	67	65	70
88.	hadn't ought	46	46	45	47	43	42	38	48	55	46
	oughtn't	54	54	55	53	57	58	62	52	45	54

		socioeconomic class of informants			gender of informants		age of informants				
term	variants	upper	middle	lower	male	female	< 20	20-40	40-60	> 60	ALL
89.	didn't used to	100	100	98	99	99	100	100	100	97	100
	usen't	0	0	1	1	0	0	0	0	1	0
	usen't to	0	0	1	0	1	0	0	0	1	0
90.	a + participle	0	0	0	0	0	0	0	0	0	0
91.	going	100	100	100	100	100	100	100	100	100	100
92.	rottening	0	16	31	16	16	12	8	18	25	16
	rotting	100	84	69	84	84	88	92	82	75	84
93.	to tell	100	100	100	100	100	100	100	100	100	100
94.	might could	0	0	0	0	0	0	0	0	0	0
95.	wants in	74	92	100	89	88	83	88	90	92	89
	...to come in	26	8	0	11	12	17	12	10	8	11

		socioeconomic class of informants			gender of informants		age of informants				
term	variants	upper	middle	lower	male	female	< 20	20-40	40-60	> 60	ALL
96.	wants off	51	46	86	62	62	52	58	65	70	61
	...to get off	49	54	14	38	38	48	42	35	30	39
97.	wants out	74	92	100	89	88	83	88	90	93	89
	...to go out	26	8	0	11	12	17	12	10	7	11
98.	at	100	100	100	100	100	100	100	100	100	100
99.	on	100	100	100	100	100	100	100	100	100	100
100.	past	100	100	100	100	100	100	100	100	100	100
101.	at	100	100	100	100	100	100	100	100	100	100
102.	...for sure	0	1	6	3	3	0	0	1	8	3
	...sure	100	99	94	97	97	100	100	99	92	97
103.	after	0	5	21	10	8	15	13	12	15	14
	for	100	95	79	90	92	85	87	88	85	86

term	variants	socioeconomic class of informants			gender of informants		age of informants				
		upper	middle	lower	male	female	< 20	20-40	40-60	> 60	ALL
104.	of	35	6	0	13	8	15	13	12	15	14
	till	1	20	63	33	23	15	22	25	50	32
	to	64	74	37	54	69	70	65	63	35	54
105.	get	100	100	94	97	98	100	100	97	95	98
	take	0	0	6	3	2	0	0	3	5	2
106.	at	0	4	10	5	4	0	5	3	10	5
	to	100	96	90	95	96	100	95	97	90	95
107.	on	100	100	100	100	100	100	100	100	100	100
108.	in	100	100	100	100	100	100	100	100	100	100
109.	for	70	49	29	47	52	53	65	38	43	49
	on	30	51	71	53	48	47	35	62	57	51
110.	in	100	100	100	100	100	100	100	100	100	100

Lexicon

term	variants	socioeconomic class of informants			gender of informants		age of informants				
		upper	middle	lower	male	female	< 20	20-40	40-60	> 60	ALL
1.	cantaloupe	100	99	96	97	100	100	100	100	100	100
	muskmelon	0	1	4	3	0	0	0	0	0	0
2.	jam	0	0	1	1	0	0	0	0	2	0
	jelly	99	84	78	88	85	93	90	83	80	87
	marmelade	1	0	1	0	2	0	0	2	2	1
	preserves	0	16	20	11	13	7	10	15	17	12
3.	jelly	80	43	30	58	46	55	55	50	43	51
	preserves	0	16	20	11	13	7	10	15	17	12
4.	frosting	19	19	20	20	18	18	15	18	25	19
	icing	81	81	80	80	82	82	85	82	75	81

		socioeconomic class of informants			gender of informants		age of informants				
term	variants	upper	middle	lower	male	female	< 20	20-40	40-60	> 60	ALL
5.	corn...cob	100	98	95	97	97	100	100	98	92	97
	sweet corn	0	2	5	3	3	0	0	2	8	3
6.	cornbread	100	100	100	100	100	100	100	100	100	100
7.	cottage cheese	100	100	100	100	100	100	100	100	100	100
8.	doughnut	100	100	100	100	100	100	100	100	100	100
9.	float	1	5	10	7	5	0	3	7	13	6
	ice cream float	7	8	10	12	5	0	3	23	7	17
	ice cream soda	88	83	72	75	84	100	88	63	67	80
	soda	1	5	8	7	6	0	5	7	13	6
10.	hotcakes	1	5	8	8	3	0	0	10	13	6
	pancakes	99	95	92	92	97	100	100	90	87	94
11.	snack	100	100	100	100	100	100	100	100	100	100

term	variants	socioeconomic class of informants			gender of informants		age of informants				ALL
		upper	middle	lower	male	female	< 20	20-40	40-60	> 60	
12.	soda	83	81	83	85	79	95	87	75	72	83
	soda pop	17	19	17	15	21	5	13	25	28	17
13.	club	24	16	21	18	23	32	28	12	8	20
	dagwood	0	11	15	10	8	0	0	13	22	9
	hero	16	16	21	22	15	8	20	20	23	18
	poor boy	25	21	11	19	19	7	17	25	28	19
	submarine	35	35	31	31	37	53	35	30	18	34
14.	green bean	10	18	24	18	16	27	22	12	8	17
	string bean	90	82	76	82	84	73	78	88	92	83
15.	wishbone	100	100	100	100	100	100	100	100	100	100
16.	pit	75	66	58	64	68	70	67	67	62	66
	seed	25	34	42	36	32	30	33	33	38	34

term	variants	socioeconomic class of informants			gender of informants		age of informants				
		upper	middle	lower	male	female	< 20	20-40	40-60	> 60	ALL
17.	pit	15	24	24	26	18	13	20	27	28	28
	seed	85	76	76	74	82	87	80	73	72	72
18.	husks	15	19	14	17	15	5	15	20	23	16
	shucks	85	81	86	83	85	95	85	80	77	84
19.	hull	7	5	11	9	7	0	0	5	27	8
	shell	93	95	89	91	93	100	100	95	73	92
20.	drinking fount.	90	88	90	93	86	100	85	90	82	89
	water cooler	10	12	10	7	14	0	15	10	18	11
21.	chipmunk	100	100	100	100	100	100	100	100	100	100
22.	crawdad	18	53	73	52	43	43	48	45	52	48
	crawfish	46	31	23	33	34	25	38	37	33	33
	crayfish	36	16	5	16	23	32	13	18	15	19

term	variants	socioeconomic class of informants			gender of informants		age of informants				
		upper	middle	lower	male	female	< 20	20-40	40-60	> 60	ALL
23.	dragonfly	100	100	100	100	100	100	100	100	100	100
24.	earthworm	11	11	1	3	13	0	3	12	17	8
	worm	89	89	99	97	87	100	97	88	83	82
25.	firefly	6	4	3	3	5	0	2	5	10	4
	lightning bug	94	96	97	97	95	100	98	95	90	96
26.	minnow	100	100	100	100	100	100	100	100	100	100
27.	night crawler	100	100	100	100	100	100	100	100	100	100
28.	skunk	100	100	100	100	100	100	100	100	100	100
29.	brook	6	4	4	4	5	3	2	7	7	5
	creek	59	84	93	80	82	72	85	77	80	78
	stream	35	12	4	16	13	15	13	17	13	17

term	variants	socioeconomic class of informants			gender of informants		age of informants				ALL
		upper	middle	lower	male	female	< 20	20-40	40-60	> 60	
30.	cloudburst	9	14	9	11	10	8	8	10	15	10
	downpour	91	86	91	89	90	92	92	90	85	90
31.	humid	80	68	71	73	73	85	80	68	58	75
	muggy	12	20	17	17	16	12	10	23	20	16
	sticky	8	12	12	10	12	3	10	8	22	11
32.	hard maple	12	16	11	16	11	0	13	20	20	13
	sugar maple	88	84	89	84	89	100	87	80	80	87
33.	bull	100	100	100	100	100	100	100	100	100	100
34.	mixed breed	5	3	5	3	5	0	0	3	13	4
	mongrel	29	44	36	37	34	40	37	38	30	36
	mutt	66	54	59	60	61	60	63	58	57	60

term	variants	socioeconomic class of informants			gender of informants		age of informants				
		upper	middle	lower	male	female	< 20	20-40	40-60	> 60	ALL
35.	pig pen	76	79	79	74	82	100	85	73	53	78
	pig sty	24	21	21	26	18	0	15	27	47	22
36.	moo	100	100	100	100	100	100	100	100	100	100
37.	ram	100	100	100	100	100	100	100	100	100	100
38.	neigh	81	81	75	83	76	100	82	67	68	79
	whinny	19	19	25	17	24	0	18	33	32	21
39.	blinds	100	100	100	100	100	100	100	100	100	100
40.	bureau	3	1	3	3	2	0	0	2	7	2
	chest of draw.	69	69	69	63	74	43	67	80	85	69
	dresser	29	30	29	34	24	57	33	18	8	29
41.	closet	96	96	96	97	95	100	100	98	87	96
	clothes closet	4	4	4	3	5	0	0	2	13	4

term	variants	socioeconomic class of informants			gender of informants		age of informants				ALL
		upper	middle	lower	male	female	< 20	20-40	40-60	> 60	
42.	chimney	80	80	70	28	25	93	87	70	57	77
	flue	20	20	30	72	75	7	13	30	43	23
43.	bucket	97	100	100	99	99	100	100	98	98	99
	pail	3	0	0	1	1	0	0	2	2	1
44.	bucket	100	100	100	100	100	100	100	100	100	100
45.	clean up	96	93	94	94	94	100	97	88	92	94
	tidy up	4	7	6	6	6	0	3	12	8	6
46.	spiderweb	100	100	100	100	100	100	100	100	100	100
47.	cobweb	53	53	55	53	53	45	58	53	57	53
	spiderweb	47	47	45	47	47	55	42	47	43	47
48.	cobweb	66	60	76	70	65	33	63	88	85	68
	spiderweb	34	40	24	30	35	67	37	12	15	32

		socioeconomic class of informants			gender of informants		age of informants				
term	variants	upper	middle	lower	male	female	< 20	20-40	40-60	> 60	ALL
49.	dust	94	96	96	97	93	98	95	85	100	95
	dustballs	3	1	1	1	2	2	5	0	0	2
	lint	4	5	3	3	5	0	0	15	0	3
50.	faucet	100	100	100	100	100	100	100	100	100	100
51.	faucet	100	100	100	100	100	100	100	100	100	100
52.	frying pan	91	91	86	92	88	100	100	83	75	90
	skillet	9	9	14	8	12	0	0	17	25	10
53.	front room	6	4	0	4	2	0	0	3	10	3
	living room	94	96	100	96	98	100	100	97	90	97
54.	gutters	95	96	94	98	93	100	100	97	83	95
	water troughs	5	4	6	2	7	0	0	3	17	5

term	variants	socioeconomic class of informants			gender of informants		age of informants				
		upper	middle	lower	male	female	< 20	20-40	40-60	> 60	ALL
55.	outdoor toilet	15	0	0	6	4	0	8	12	0	5
	outhouse	81	97	100	93	93	100	92	88	92	93
	privy	4	3	0	2	2	0	0	0	8	2
56.	front porch	100	100	78	94	91	97	92	93	88	93
	stoop	0	0	22	6	9	3	8	7	12	7
57.	fruit cellar	96	86	85	88	90	100	95	88	73	89
	root cellar	4	14	15	12	10	0	5	12	27	11
58.	fridge	24	13	14	16	18	25	63	10	8	17
	icebox	16	21	24	20	21	5	10	30	37	20
	refrigerator	60	66	63	64	62	70	67	60	55	63
59.	couch	94	90	92	100	84	98	93	83	93	92
	sofa	6	10	8	0	16	2	7	17	7	8

term	variants	socioeconomic class of informants			gender of informants		age of informants				
		upper	middle	lower	male	female	< 20	20-40	40-60	> 60	ALL
60.	horse	1	4	6	7	1	8	7	0	0	4
	sawbuck	3	8	9	11	2	0	0	12	13	6
	sawhorse	96	88	85	82	97	92	93	88	87	80
61.	bag	53	67	67	60	68	60	73	63	60	63
	paper bag	47	30	30	38	31	40	25	37	35	36
	sack	0	3	3	2	1	0	2	0	5	2
62.	trashcan	49	50	50	53	46	57	48	45	48	50
	wastecan	51	50	50	47	54	43	52	55	52	50
63.	garbage can	18	20	14	16	18	0	10	17	42	17
	trash can	82	80	86	84	82	100	90	83	58	83

		socioeconomic class of informants			gender of informants		age of informants				
term	variants	upper	middle	lower	male	female	< 20	20-40	40-60	> 60	ALL
64.	dad	94	96	98	96	96	93	93	97	100	96
	daddy	4	1	1	0	4	7	2	0	0	2
	father	2	3	1	4	0	0	5	3	0	2
65.	mom	3	94	96	96	93	97	90	90	100	94
	mommy	1	1	0	0	2	3	0	0	0	1
	mother	6	5	4	4	6	0	10	10	0	5
66.	hillbilly	0	1	0	0	1	0	0	0	2	0
	hoosier	100	99	100	100	99	100	100	100	100	100

		socioeconomic class of informants			gender of informants		age of informants				
term	variants	upper	middle	lower	male	female	< 20	20-40	40-60	> 60	ALL
67.	black	65	65	59	57	69	100	62	43	47	63
	colored	9	6	10	8	9	0	8	12	13	8
	coon	3	3	3	2	3	0	3	5	2	3
	negro	14	10	10	14	8	0	13	10	22	11
	nigger	0	3	4	2	2	0	0	0	8	2
	spook	10	14	15	17	9	0	13	30	8	13
68	coon	10	11	3	3	0	0	0	2	3	1
	hillbilly	0	1	0	1	0	0	0	0	2	0
	hoosier	43	44	50	46	56	43	43	55	45	50
	nigger	44	50	41	47	43	52	52	40	39	45
	spook	3	4	6	3	1	5	5	3	3	4

		socioeconomic class of informants			gender of informants		age of informants				
term	variants	upper	middle	lower	male	female	< 20	20-40	40-60	> 60	ALL
69.	cop	43	56	61	58	48	55	62	48	48	53
	fuzz	0	1	0	1	0	0	2	0	0	0
	pig	0	0	4	2	1	3	2	0	0	1
	policeman	58	43	35	40	51	42	35	52	52	45
70.	relations	1	0	0	1	0	0	0	0	2	0
	relatives	99	100	100	99	100	100	100	100	98	100
71.	guys	55	51	53	53	53	55	48	55	53	53
	you guys	44	49	46	45	48	45	52	42	47	46
	youse guys	1	0	1	2	0	0	0	3	0	1
72.	fire house	56	55	50	54	53	57	55	50	53	9
	fire station	44	45	50	46	47	43	45	50	47	91

		socioeconomic class of informants			gender of informants		age of informants				
term	variants	upper	middle	lower	male	female	< 20	20-40	40-60	> 60	ALL
73.	fire hydrant	40	43	46	41	45	27	17	70	58	43
	fire plug	18	16	14	18	13	12	13	13	25	16
74.	seesaw	90	89	89	91	88	100	95	80	78	89
	teeter totter	10	11	11	9	12	0	5	20	22	11
75.	eighteen-whlr.	30	26	28	27	29	5	47	50	10	28
	Mack truck	18	19	29	19	24	7	38	38	3	22
	semi	30	26	28	27	29	5	47	50	10	28
	tractor-trailer	24	25	20	23	23	0	7	5	80	23
76.	dock	81	78	76	83	73	78	78	78	78	78
	pier	18	21	23	16	25	22	22	22	17	20
	wharf	1	1	1	1	2	0	0	0	5	1

term	variants	socioeconomic class of informants			gender of informants		age of informants				
		upper	middle	lower	male	female	< 20	20-40	40-60	> 60	ALL
77.	belly bumper	20	16	13	14	18	17	22	20	7	16
	belly buster	79	84	86	86	80	83	78	80	90	83
	belly flop	1	0	1	0	2	0	0	0	3	1
78.	belly buster	16	19	25	24	16	12	23	23	22	20
	belly flop	84	81	75	76	84	88	77	77	78	80
79.	belch	35	68	89	68	59	58	62	63	72	64
	burp	65	32	11	32	41	42	38	37	28	36
80.	catty-corner	100	100	98	98	100	100	100	100	97	99
	kitty-corner	0	0	2	2	0	0	0	0	3	1
81.	escort	10	0	0	0	7	0	0	0	13	3
	take	90	100	100	100	93	100	100	100	87	97

		socioeconomic class of informants			gender of informants		age of informants				
term	variants	upper	middle	lower	male	female	< 20	20-40	40-60	> 60	ALL
82.	favors	0	4	9	4	4	0	0	10	7	4
	looks like	64	60	40	54	55	57	52	57	53	55
83.	crawl	100	100	100	100	100	100	100	100	100	100
84.	look after	0	0	9	2	4	0	0	5	7	3
85.	brought up	0	0	10	3	4	0	0	8	5	3
	raised	100	100	90	97	96	100	100	92	95	97
86.	be truant	20	8	1	5	14	0	7	15	17	10
	play hookey	35	45	53	45	43	0	40	67	70	44
	skip	31	31	30	32	30	100	12	8	3	31
	skip class	4	5	5	6	3	0	13	5	0	5
	skip school	10	11	11	13	11	0	28	5	10	11

		socioeconomic class of informants			gender of informants		age of informants				
term	variants	upper	middle	lower	male	female	< 20	20-40	40-60	> 60	ALL
87.	long way	24	25	20	25	21	27	18	23	23	23
	long ways	76	75	80	75	79	73	82	77	77	77
88.	slick	35	46	64	49	48	48	43	50	52	48
	slippery	65	54	36	51	52	52	57	50	48	52
89.	binoculars	58	63	53	58	57	98	90	22	20	58
	field glasses	42	37	47	42	43	2	10	78	80	42
90.	casket	34	48	71	53	48	47	47	55	55	51
	coffin	66	52	39	47	52	53	53	45	45	49
91.	grease job	33	63	65	51	56	50	52	52	60	53
	greased	67	38	28	46	43	50	45	43	38	44
	lube job	0	0	8	3	2	0	3	5	2	3

		socioeconomic class of informants			gender of informants		age of informants				
term	variants	upper	middle	lower	male	female	< 20	20-40	40-60	> 60	ALL
92.	harmonica	96	94	93	94	94	100	100	98	95	94
	mouth harp	4	6	7	6	6	0	0	2	5	6
93.	baby buggy	81	94	93	88	90	100	100	82	75	89
	baby carriage	8	3	4	5	4	0	0	10	8	5
	carriage	11	4	4	7	6	0	0	8	17	6
94.	bathing suit	13	13	0	0	17	0	0	17	17	8
	swim suit	73	71	78	81	67	98	77	58	62	74
	swim trunks	15	16	22	19	17	2	23	25	22	18
95.	sled	75	76	63	78	64	72	70	73	70	71
	sleigh	25	24	37	22	36	28	30	27	30	29
96.	ghost	100	100	99	99	100	100	100	100	98	100
	spook	0	0	1	1	0	0	0	0	2	0

Even a cursory glance at these data indicates that the answer to the first question is resoundingly affirmative. As Table 22 makes clear, all four independent variables proved fruitful in isolating the social correlates of linguistic variation.

TABLE 22
QUANTITY OF ITEMS INVESTIGATED SHOWING PATTERNED VARIATION

		Independent variable				
Number of items investigated		SEC	Context	Gender	Age	Items showing no Variation
phonology:	46	52	52	2	30	48
morphology/ syntax:	110	64	NA	55	64	36
lexicon:	96	77	NA	61	77	23

Although a detailed analysis of each sound, morphological and syntactic form, and lexical item investigated would require far more space than can realistically be afforded them here--and is, in fact, unnecessary, since readers interested in such specifics can easily make these comparisons themselves-- several general patterns emerge from the data that can be discussed more briefly. Consider, for example, that St. Louisans perceive some pronunciations as "more correct" or "more standard" than others, as attested by the variation according to contextual formality; and consider also that in each instance there is a corresponding pattern of variation according to the socioeconomic class of the speaker. Conclusions such as these are perhaps to be expected (cf. the similar findings of Labov 1966, Wolfram 1969, and Trudgill 1974a), but it is interesting to note further that whenever there is variation according to the age of the informant, the usage of increasingly older speakers seems to parallel a decline in social class and contextual formality. Put another way, the older a Gateway City speaker becomes, the farther short he or she falls from hitting the stylistic ideal aimed at.

Regarding the morphological forms, two patterns identical to the ones noted above emerge: first, there is a clear correlation between decreased socioeconomic status and increased use of nonstandard conjugations; second, an increase in age also typically parallels an increase in the use of such conjugations, and especially so for speakers over the age of 60. And when there is variation according to the gender of the speakers, males far more often than females tend to use the nonstandard forms (cf. the conslusions of Labov 1972: 243; Trudgill 1974a: 93–94 and 1974b: 84–102; and Wolfram and Shuy 1974: 93–94). Furthermore, a number of more minor patterns can be noted that follow closely the findings of Atwood in his *Survey of Verb Forms in the Eastern United States* (1953). To begin, the preterite and past participle forms of verbs often level to a single construction, especially among the members of the lower class (thus, for example, ***broke***, ***done***, ***drank***, ***drunk***, ***drove***, ***rid***, ***rode***, ***seen***, ***shrunk***, ***swelled***, ***swum***, and ***wore*** all occur frequently), and this construction is usually the standard preterite of the verb in question (cf. Atwood 1953: 43). Moreover, some preterites and participles of verbs ending in *–t* level to the present indicative tense (e.g., ***fit***, which appears to be the standard in St. Louis, as well as ***knit*** and ***sweat***; cf. Atwood 1953: 44). And many uninflected forms (e.g., ***come***, ***give***, and ***run***) "have more or less currency in popular but not in cultured speech" (Atwood 1953: 44). Atwood also lists the following verbs as "popular" favorites that are "extensive in the noncultured types but relatively uncommon among the cultured" (1953: 41), a contention that my data strongly support: ***bit*** 'bitten,' ***broke*** 'broken,' ***done*** 'did,' ***drug*** 'dragged,' ***kneeled*** 'knelt,' ***rode*** 'ridden,' ***rung*** 'rang,' ***seen*** 'saw,' ***swelled*** 'swollen,' ***tore*** 'torn,' and ***wore*** 'worn'. Finally, ***hadn't ought***, which Atwood says is sometimes used in cultured speech, as well as ***dasn't***, ***here's your clothes***, and ***laid*** 'lay', which he says are often used by as many as one–half of the cultured speakers (1953: 41), also occur in similar proportions in my data.

A consideration of syntactic forms and lexical items is a bit more problematic, for they are not typically regarded as "standard" or "nonstandard" except in particular geographic areas (which can at times be quite localized), and thus do not lend themselves to easy analysis. Yet the data show a surprisingly high percentage of patterns parallel to the socioeconomic class, gender, and age of the speaker, so some attempt at explanation is clearly necessary. In Table 23 I have collected all of the forms in my data (including verb tenses and pronunciation, for purposes of comparison) that are favored by a majority of all the St. Louisans surveyed and that have been linked conclusively to one or more of the five major dialect areas in the United States (North, South, Midlands, North Midland, and South Midland) or have been classed as "in general use" or "urban" by Kurath's *Word Geography* (1949), Atwood's *Survey of Verb Forms* (1953), or Kurath and McDavid's *Pronunciation of English* (1961).[1]

Curiously, perhaps, the North and North Midland areas are represented much more heavily than are the South and South Midland areas (49 percent versus 20 percent overall, 55 percent versus 21 percent for morphological/syntactic and lexical items only), indicating that most St. Louisans perceive more Northern and North Midland forms as "standard" than they do Southern and South Midland forms. Because this trend will figure so prominently in my answer to the third question below, I will reserve extensive comment until later; suffice it to say that it is extremely interesting that St. Louisans should have these region–related perceptions of "standardness" and "nonstrandardness."

2. How does the language of St. Louis compare to known dialectal patterns in the eastern United States, in Missouri, and in Illinois?

This question can best be answered if it is first divided into its logical parts. Beginning with the known dialectal patterns in Missouri, we can further distinguish between those of the state as a whole and those of just the St. Louis area. Johnson's master's thesis, "A Brief Study of Dialect in St. Louis" (1976), is the only extensive analysis of language variation in the Gateway City that I know of, and as I noted in Chapter 1, his extremely small number of informants (n = 11) somewhat limits the validity of his conclusions. Nevertheless, Table 24 shows all of the linguistic forms investigated by Johnson (for which he provides conclusive results) that also appear in the present study, along with the relevant indices of usage by all informants.

What is especially interesting here is the remarkable similarity between some of Johnson's and my indices: those for quarter *to* the hour are identical, those for *seesaw* and *teeter totter* nearly so, and the range of scores allowed by Johnson's "frequent," "occasional," and "general" labels easily include the percentages I report for *greasy* (both [s] and [z]), *couch*, *creek*, *pancakes*, *dragonfly*, and *gutters*. Moreover, although many of Johnson's and my indices appear not to be at all similar, it is noteworthy that the relative rankings of variants for a given phonological item or semantic category are usually the same. Thus while I report a percentage of 99 for *bucket* and 1 for *pail* as opposed to Johnson's 91 and 18—apparently dissimilar scores—the vast majority of both groups of informants

TABLE 23
ITEMS INVESTIGATED THAT CAN BE LINKED TO MAJOR DIALECT AREAS OF THE UNITED STATES*

Item investigated	N	N+NM	NM	M	SM	SM+S	S	N+S	General use	Urban
postvocalic [r]				x						
[r] in quarter							x			
[w] (whip, etc.)				x			x			
[hj] (humor)								x		
[j] (humor)				x			x			
vcd. interd. (with(out))	x									
vcels. interd. (with(out))				x						
intrusive [r]				x						
[s] (grease, greasy)		x								
[j] (yeast)	x									
[mIsIz] (Mrs.)		x								
mid-front lax vowel (pen)	x			x						

TABLE 23 (cont.)

Item investigated	N	N+NM	NM	M	SM	SM+S	S	N+S	General use	Urban
low-back vowel (log, fog)				x			x			
low-back vowel (foreign)		x								
mid-front lax vowel (Mary, marry, merry)				x						
high-front lax vowel (stomach)				x						
diphthong (bite)		x								
diphthong (house)			x							
[u] (roof)							x			
low-back vowel (hearth)				x						
schwa (because)	x									
[o] (pre-r)		x								
low-back vowel (pre-r)	x									
[u] (due, etc.)		x								

TABLE 23 (cont.)

Item investigated	N	N+NM	NM	M	SM	SM+S	S	N+S	General use	Urban
mid-front lax vowel (catch)						x				
[i] (creek)	x					x				
low-back vowel (sausage)	x									
[i] (Missouri)										x
[o] (potato)	x									
schwa (potato)				x			x			
dove (past of to dive)	x									
hadn't ought	x									
wants off				x						
quarter to (the hour)								x		
sick to (the stomach)	x									
wait on (someone)				x						
corn on the cob		x								

TABLE 23 (cont.)

Item investigated	N	N+NM	NM	M	SM	SM+S	S	N+S	General use	Urban
cornbread									x	
cottage cheese									x	
doughnut									x	
snack									x	
string bean		x								
(cherry) pit		x								
(peach) seed				x						
(corn) shucks						x				
shell (beans)								x		
chipmunk		x								
earthworm									x	
skunk		x								
wishbone		x								
bull	x									
moo		x								
blinds				x						

TABLE 23 (cont.)

Item investigated	N	N+NM	NM	M	SM	SM+S	S	N+S	General use	Urban
bucket (tin)						x				
bucket (wood)						x				
faucet	x									
gutters									x	
outhouse	x									
(paper) bag	x									
belly buster (on snow)		x								
(baby) crawls				x						
play hookey		x								
baby buggy				x						
	N	N+NM	NM	M	SM	SM+S	S	N+S	General use	Urban
TOTALS	16	14	2	17	0	4	7	3	7	1

*Based on the preferences of the majority of all St. Louisans investigated. If phonetic variants occur in free variation or if the alternate variants of any given form are favored approximately equally, both variants are given.

TABLE 24
A COMPARISON OF THE FINDINGS OF THE PRESENT STUDY WITH THOSE OF JOHNSON (1976) (%)

Item investigated	Present study (n = 240)	Johnson (1976) (n = 11)
greasy [s]	57	"frequent"[a]
greasy [z]	43	"occasional"[b]
Mary (mid-front lax vowel)	100	"frequent"
Mary ([e])	0	"occasional"
tomato(es) [o]	51	"frequent"
tomato(es) (schwa)	49	"occasional"
wash [r]	73	"frequent"
quarter of (the hour)	14	27
quarter till (the hour)	32	18
quarter to (the hour)	54	54
sick at (the stomach)	5	18
sick to (the stomach)	95	82
bucket	99	91
pail	1	18

TABLE 24 (cont.)

Item investigated	Present study (n = 240)	Johnson (1976) (n = 11)
firefly[c]	4	36
green bean	17	45
string bean	83	55
hull (beans)[d]	8	27
(corn) husks	16	55
(corn) shucks	84	36
couch	92	"general"[e]
creek	78	"general"
stream	17	"general"
pancakes	94	"general"
dragonfly	100	"general"
gutters	95	"general"
seesaw	89	91
teeter totter	11	9

TABLE 24 (cont.)

[a] Johnson uses "frequent" to refer to from six to seven occurances, or 55-64%.

[b] Johnson uses "occasional" to refer to from three to five occurances, or 27-45%.

[c] Johnson does not list *lightning bug*, but presumably most of the rest of his informants gave this response.

[d] Johnson does not list *shell* (beans), but presumably the rest of his informants gave this response.

[e] Johnson lists as "general" all those terms that "are in general use in [the] St. Louis area" (1976: 67).

---

obviously prefer *bucket*, with only a slim minority favoring *pail*. Similarly, by far most of our informants get sick *to* rather than *at* the stomach and eat *string beans* rather than *green beans*, and these facts should not be overlooked through simple comparisons of numbers. Indeed, the only serious discrepancies between Johnson's and my data appear to lie in "quarter *of/till* the hour" (my informants prefer *till* by a margin of 2:1, and Johnson's favor *of* by 3:2), *husks/shucks* (my informants prefer *shucks* overwhelmingly, but slightly more than half of Johnson's use *husks*), and *stream* (which only a comparatively small percentage of my informants use, but which Johnson lists as "general"). Table 25 contains a summary of the similarities and differences between the results of Johnson's and my research. Although it is difficult to explain the entries in the "discrepancies" column, I suspect that if Johnson had used a larger sample of informants, his results would have been more comparable to my own.

For Missouri as a whole, comprehensive analyses of phonology and morphology do not exist; however, the Ph.D. dissertation written by Faries, "A Word Geography of Missouri" (1967), allows a detailed comparison of my syntactic and lexical data with those collected from the rest of the state. In Table 26 I have collected all of the forms that appear in both Faries's and my research, and have

TABLE 25
A SUMMARY OF THE SIMILARITIES AND DIFFERENCES BETWEEN THE FINDINGS OF THE PRESENT STUDY AND THOSE OF JOHNSON (1976)

	similarities[a]		same relative usage status[b]		discrepancies[c]	
	n	%	n	%	n	%
phonology:	3	43	4	57	0	0
morphology/ syntax	1	20	2	40	2	40
lexicon	3	19	10	63	3	19
total forms	7	25	16	57	5	18

[a] Indices were counted as similar if they were within 10 percentage points of each other and conformed to the same pattern of relative usage status (see note b).

[b] Variants were counted as having the same relative usage status if their usage relative to the usage of the other variants was constant; that is, for example, if semantic category A produced variants x, y, and z, and if the rank ordering of variants for the other group of informants was x-y-z and the rank ordering of variants for the other group of informants was z-y-x, variant y would be counted as having the same relative usage status while variants x and z would not.

[c] Indices were labeled as being discrepancies if they did not conform to the same pattern of relative usage status (see note b).

TABLE 25 (cont.)

SPECIAL NOTE: Indices from Johnson's "frequent" and "occasional" labels were computed as the averages of his allowable ranges (thus "frequent" was counted as 59.5, or the average of 55 and 64, and "occasional" was counted as 36, or the average of 27 and 45), and all of his "general" labels were computed as being in the range 75-100. (Except for *stream*, which was tallied as a discrepancy, all of the forms labeled "general" were counted as having the same relative usage status but not being withn 10 percentage points of each other.)

TABLE 26
A COMPARISON OF THE FINDINGS OF THE PRESENT STUDY WITH THOSE OF FARIES (1967) (%)

	Present study (n = 240)		Faries (1967) (n = 700)[a]
Item investigated	all	aged 60-80	all "elderly"
quarter of (the hour)	14	15	16
quarter to (the hour)	54	35	22
quarter till (the hour)	32	50	62
sick at the stomach	5	10	83*
sick to the stomach	95	90	6*

TABLE 26 (cont.)

Item investigated	Present study (n = 240) all	aged 60-80	Faries (1967) (n = 700)[a] all "elderly"
sick to the stomach	95	90	6*
wants off	61	70	47*
wants to get off	39	30	50
front room	3	10	20
living room	97	90	65
blinds	100	100	60*
clothes closet	4	13	99*
gutters	95	83	55
water troughs	5	17	6
outdoor toilet	5	0	24*
outhouse	93	92	"infrequent use"
privy	2	8	10
faucet	100	100	92
bucket (tin)	99	98	86*
bucket (wood)	100	100	85*

TABLE 26 (cont.)

Item investigated	Present study (n = 240) all	aged 60-80	Faries (1967) (n = 700)[a] all "elderly"
pail	1	2	21
frying pan[b]	90	75	15
skillet[b]	10	25	93
(paper) bag	99	95	80
(paper) sack	2	5	10
seesaw	89	78	45
teeter totter	11	22	64*
sawbuck	6	13	50*
sawhorse	80	87	45
brook	5	7	5
creek	78	80	70
bull	100	100	75
moo	100	100	87*
whinny	21	32	23
neigh	79	68	"a few"

TABLE 26 (cont.)

Item investigated	Present study (n = 240) all	aged 60-80	Faries (1967) (n = 700)[a] all "elderly"
wishbone	100	100	47
cornbread	100	100	95
doughnut	100	100	95+
hotcakes	6	13	11
pancakes	94	87	75
cottage cheese	100	100	70
snack	100	100	77*
(to) hull (beans)	8	27	67*
(to) shell (beans)	92	73	35
green bean	17	8	66*
string bean	83	92	37*
(corn) husks	16	23	14*
(corn) shucks	84	77	87*
corn on the cob	97	92	0*
sweet corn	3	8	15

TABLE 26 (cont.)

Item investigated	Present study (n = 240) all	aged 60-80	Faries (1967) (n = 700)[a] all "elderly"
skunk	100	100	69*
chipmunk	100	100	32*
earthworm	8	17	8*
dragonfly	100	100	10*
firefly	4	10	5*
lightning bug	96	90	95
hard maple	13	20	13*
sugar maple	87	80	65
baby buggy	89	75	90*
baby carriage	5	8	16*
play hookey	44	70	79*
be/play truant	10	17	7*
skip school	11	10	25
belly bump(er) (snow)	16	7	15*

TABLE 26 (cont.)

Item investigated	Present study (n = 240) all	aged 60-80	Faries (1967) (n = 700)[a] all "elderly"
belly bust (er)	83	90	50*
belly flop(per) (snow)	1	3	3*
take (someone home)	97	87	95
porch	93	88	90
stoop	7	12	12*

[a] The figure of 700 here is approximate. Because Faries sometimes recorded more than a single response from the same informant and sometimes recorded no response, those percentages marked with an asterisk (which I have calculated based on Faries's raw scores and using 700 as the total number possible) may be slightly low or high.

[b] Faries stipulated that the item in question here was made of "cast iron"; I described the item as made of "metal, perhaps with a non-stick surface."

also supplied the relevant corresponding indices of usage (both the "aged 60 to 80" and the "total average" indices are included from the present study because Faries describes all of her informants as being "elderly").

Although there are many similarities here (cf., e.g., the indices for "quarter *of* [the hour]," *privy, faucet, creek, cornbread, doughnut, hotcakes, firefly, lightning bug, hard maple, belly bump*[*er*], *belly flop*[*per*], *porch*, and *stoop*) and also many apparent dissimilarities that nevertheless have the same relative rankings for usage preference by informants (e.g., *front room* and *living room*, *bucket* [tin and wood] and *pail, pancakes, cottage cheese, skunk, sugar maple, skip school*, and *belly bust*[*er*]), one is also struck by the large number of discrepancies. Almost all St. Louisans, for example, want *off* the bus when they get sick *to* the stomach whereas other Missourians want *to get off* the bus when they get sick *at* the stomach. Similarly, most St. Louisans either use or recall using the *seesaw* at the playground, but elsewhere in Missouri *teeter totter* is preferred; and though most St. Louis horses *neigh*, only "a few" neigh in other parts of the state. Moreover, St. Louisans tend to *shell* their *string beans* and perhaps serve them with *corn on the cob* whereas residents of other parts of the state usually *hull* their *green beans* and almost never serve *corn on the cob*. Finally, while *chipmunks* and *dragonflies* are commonplace in the Gateway City, they are obviously known by other names almost everywhere else in Missouri. Both St. Louis and Missouri may be located in the Midland dialect area, but Table 26 suggests that St. Louis has more of a North/North Midland orientation and the state as a whole is more heavily South/South Midland. Table 27 contains a summary of the similarities and differences between the results of Faries's and my research.

TABLE 27
A SUMMARY OF THE SIMILARITIES AND DIFFERENCES BETWEEN THE FINDINGS OF THE PRESENT STUDY AND THOSE OF FARIES (1967)

	similarities*				same relative usage status*				discrepancies*			
	all		60-80		all		60-80		all		60-80	
	n	%	n	%	n	%	n	%	n	%	n	%
morphology/ syntax	1	7	1	7	0	0	2	14	6	43	4	29
lexicon	24	39	23	38	20	33	20	33	17	28	18	30
total forms	25	37	24	35	20	29	22	32	23	34	22	32

*This heading is explained in the notes to Table 25.

Perhaps the most notable feature of Table 27 is the relative paucity of age–related differences in usage that it depicts; indeed, the "similarities" column shows only identical or near–identical figures among Faries's "elderly" informants, my informants between the ages of 60 and 80, and my total sample––and the same is true of the "lexicon" entries in the "same relative usage status" and "discrepancies" columns and the "total forms" entries in the "discrepancies" column. Only morphological and syntactic usage in the "same relative usage status" and "discrepancies" columns and the "total forms" entries in the "same relative usage status" column appear traceable to differences in the ages of our respondents (and even in these categories the differences between Faries's figures and my own never exceed + or – 2). Speculation as to why this should be the case is difficult at best; no doubt many significant differences have been lost through the technique of averaging, but perhaps Faries's use of only elderly informants was not as severely limiting as I charged in Chapter 1.

Other comparisons of the language of St. Louis with known dialectal patterns in Missouri as well as in Illinois can be made in a more general way. Dakin (1971), for example, although working only east of the Mississippi River, projected that much of Missouri and certainly the entire city of St. Louis would fall into a dialectal area that could perhaps best be characterized as a "transitional region" that lies south of the North Midland isogloss and north of the South Midland isogloss. In this region both North Midland and South Midland linguistic forms predominate, often with co–existance in the same speech community and even the same speaker, and sometimes with no discernible preference between them. Subsequently, Lance (1974a, 1974b, 1975, 1977) has confirmed Dakin's suspicions regarding Missouri and St. Louis, calling the transitional region "ambiguously midland" (1974a: 9–10). Fig. 2 depicts this area as Lance (1977: 297, map 5) has mapped it out.

Although the Gateway City clearly falls within the bounds of this transitional area, I have already shown (and will show in greater detail shortly) that St. Louisans seem generally to favor Northern and North Midland rather than Southern and South Midland linguistic forms. This conclusion fits nicely with the findings of Frazer (1973, 1978, 1979), who, following Marckwardt (1957), confirmed the existance of a "speech island" that surrounds the St. Louis area. In this speech island, as Frazer (1979: 186) says, "the vocabulary and pronunciation are Northern and North Midland, contrasting sharply with the regional [South Midland] speech of the surrounding area." The approximate boundaries of this speech island, which, according to Frazer (1979: 192, n. 1), includes all or part of the Illinois counties of Calhoun, Madison, St. Clair, Monroe, Bond, Clinton, and Washington, and all or part of the Missouri counties of St. Louis, St. Charles, Jefferson, Franklin, Washington, Crawford, Gasconade, and Osage, are depicted in Fig. 3.

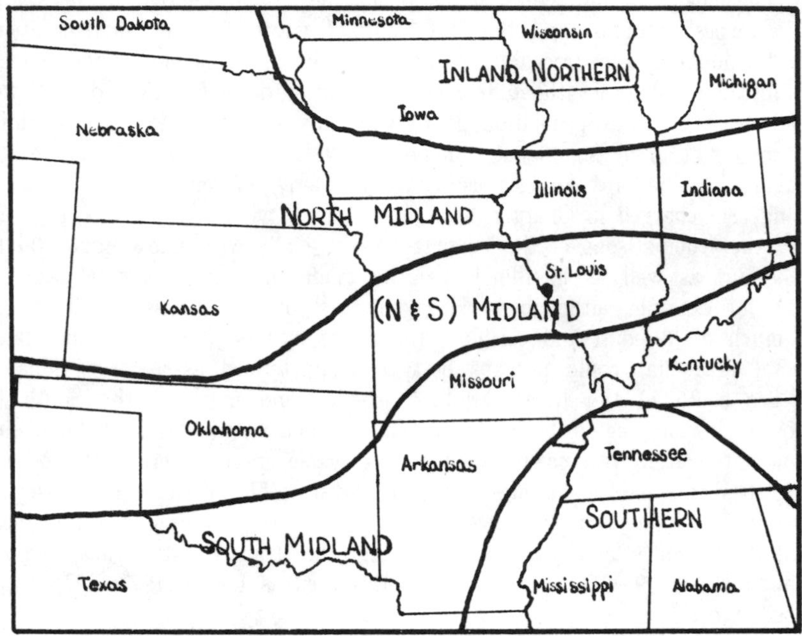

Fig. 2: The "Ambiguously Midland" Region
(based on Lance 1977: 297, map 5)

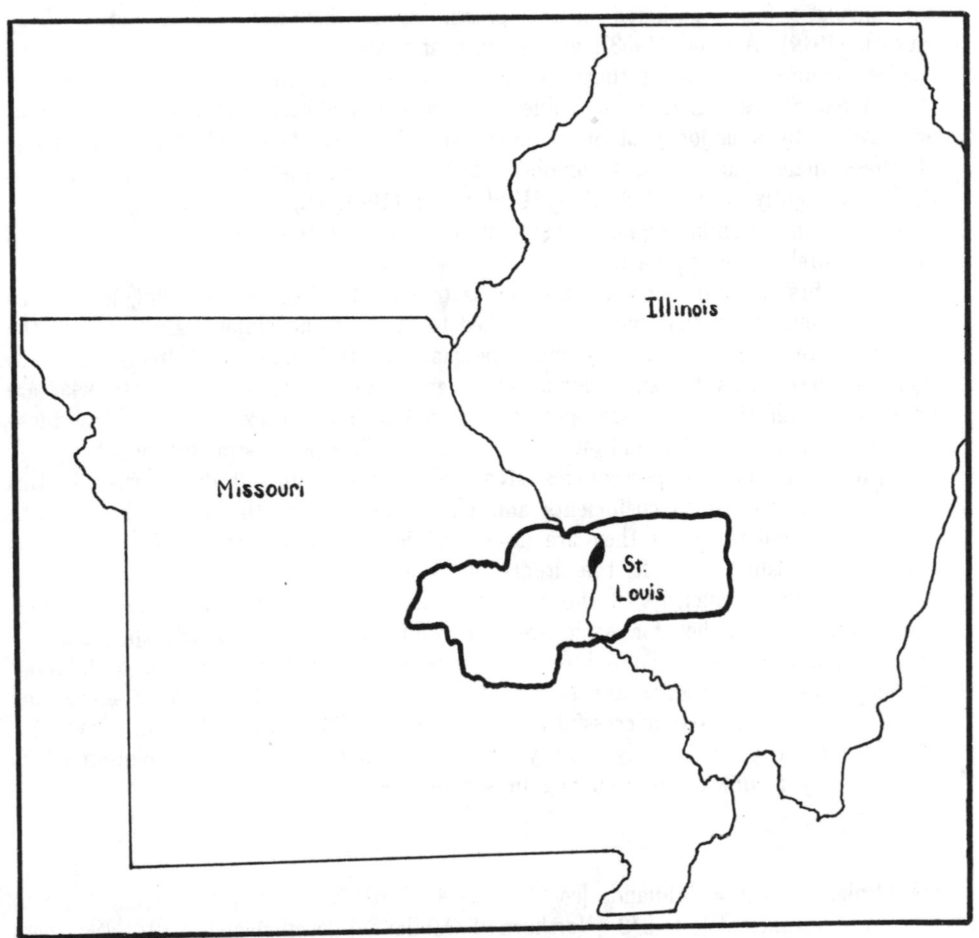

Fig. 3: The Approximate Boundaries of the Northern/North Midland Speech Island Surrounding St. Louis

Finally, a comparison of the language of St. Louis with the known dialectal patterns of the eastern United States requires a rather extensive correlation of all the linguistic forms gathered in the present study that were also investigated by Kurath (1949), Atwood (1953), and Kurath and McDavid (1961) and found to have isogloss boundaries placing them in one or more of the five major dialect areas of the United States. Earlier, in Table 23, I collected all the forms in my data that are favored by a majority of St. Louisans and that have been linked to at least one of these dialect areas––a technique which, though satisfactory for my purposes then, has rightly been criticized by Underwood (1981: 66) for "tacitly ignoring . . . variants with potential regional distribution" and will thus be replaced now by a more comprehensive approach.

The first step in such an analysis is to list all of the variant linguistic forms of the present study that have been linked to at least one major dialect area in the eastern states. Second, a tally must be made of the quantity of items linked to each of these areas for each demographic group of informants (all those who are upper class, all those who are speaking in an informal context, all males, all those between the ages of 20 and 40, and so on). This is a straightforward process requiring only that the percentages given in the regrouping of data earlier in this chapter be converted to coefficients and placed adjacent to the dialect area(s) with which the linguistic forms they are associated have been matched. When this has been accomplished for all the items in a given portion of the survey (e.g., phonology), the coefficients of the respective dialect areas are added, the end result being one usage index for each area or combination of areas (South, South + Midlands, and so on). To reduce these indices to only five––one for each major dialect area––five formulas are used that were first developed by Donald Lance and Rachel Faries and used successfully by Johnson (1976), and that I have modified slightly for the present study. They are as follows (as reported by Johnson [1976: 69], with my modifications occurring in square brackets):

(1) Midland Index = Midlands [coefficients] + North Midlands [coefficients] + South Midlands [coefficients] + 2/3 (Northern + Midlands) [coefficients] + 2/3 (Southern + Midlands) [coefficients] + 1/2 (North + North Midlands [coefficients] + 1/2 (South + South Midlands) [coefficients] [+ 1/3 "general use" coefficients]

(2) Northern Index = Northern [coefficients] + 1/2 (Northern + Southern) [coefficients] + 1/3 (Northern + Midlands) [coefficients] + 1/2 (Northern + North Midlands) [coefficients] [+ 1/3 "general use" coefficients]

(3) Southern Index = Southern [coefficients] + 1/2 (Northern + Southern) [coefficients] + 1/3 (Southern + Midlands) [coefficients] + 1/2 (Southern + South Midlands) [coefficients] [+ 1/3 "general use" coefficients]

(4) North Midlands Index = North Midlands [coefficients] + 1/2 Midlands [coefficients] + 1/3 (Northern + Midlands) [coefficients] + 1/3 (Southern + Midlands) [coefficients] + 1/2 (Northern + North Midlands) [coefficients] + 1/2 (Southern + North Midlands) [coefficients] [+ 1/6 "general use" coefficients]

(5) South Midlands Index = South Midlands [coefficients] + 1/2 Midlands [coefficients] + 1/3 (Northern + Midlands) [coefficients] + 1/3 (Southern + Midlands) [coefficients] + 1/2 (Southern + South Midlands) [coefficients] + 1/2 (Northern + South Midlands) [coefficients] [+ 1/6 "general use" coefficients)

In addition to these five indices, I have also calculated values for "urban" forms and "St. Louis only" forms (this latter for the pronunciation of ***sundae*** that has a mid–central vowel in final position).

The sum of these seven values represents the total possible regional affiliations of any major portion of the survey for any given demographic group of informants. To ascertain what percentage of that group's language is traceable to a specific dialect area, one need only divide the indices of that area into the total. The affilliations of St. Louis phonology, morphology/syntax, and lexicon with the major dialect areas of the eastern United States are presented in Tables 28, 29, and 30, respectively.

These three tables provide the clearest evidence yet for the claim that I have been making throughout this chapter––that though a Midlands city, St. Louis strongly favors the North and North Midland dialect areas rather than the South and South Midland. Indeed, with regard to the morphological/syntactic and lexical items, the Northern area outweighs even the Midlands in most demographic groups, and when combined with the North Midland, typically accounts for 40 to 50 percent of the total linguistic forms used (compared to a combined total of only 15 to 30 percent from the South and South Midland). Furthermore, and again reinforcing an earlier conclusion, linguistic usage in St. Louis is not typically balanced among the several demographic groups sampled: when variation occurs, members of the upper class, females, and younger informants tend to use Northern and North Midland forms; members of the lower class, males, and elderly informants, however, tend to use Southern and South Midland forms (cf. the similar conclusions of Lance and Slemons 1976 regarding the independent variable of age).

TABLE 28

THE AFFILLIATION OF ST. LOUIS PHONOLOGY WITH THE MAJOR DIALECT AREAS OF THE EASTERN UNITED STATES (%)

	independent variable														
dialect area	socioeconomic class of informants			contextual formality			gender of informants		age of informants						
	upper	middle	lower	informal	midformal	formal	male*	female*	< 30*	< 40*	30 to 60*	40 to 60*	< 60*	60 to 80	ALL
Midlands	25	30	29	30	31	31	35	35	28	34	29	36	35	22	28
North	16	19	16	16	19	18	17	17	18	20	17	22	16	16	17
South	14	13	14	13	12	11	13	13	9	8	9	10	10	8	13
N Midlands	22	19	21	20	20	21	24	24	22	27	23	18	28	26	21
S Midlands	15	12	15	15	13	12	11	12	11	10	11	13	11	11	13
Urban*	6	5	4	4	4	5	NA	NA	13	NA	12	2	NA	18	5
St. Louis*	1	2	2	2	2	1	NA	NA	NA	NA	NA	NA	NA	NA	2

*Figures for this demographic group or dialect area are based on extremely limited amounts of data.

TABLE 29
THE AFFILLIATIONS OF ST. LOUIS MORPHOLOGY AND SYNTAX WITH THE MAJOR DIALECT AREAS OF THE EASTERN UNITED STATES (%)

	independent variable									
	socioeconomic class of informants			gender of informants		age of informants				
dialect area	upper	middle	lower	male	female	< 20	20 to 40	40 to 60	> 60	ALL
Midlands	18	23	31	26	22	20	22	25	29	24
North	36	28	21	27	30	32	29	26	25	28
South	8	12	13	12	10	9	11	11	13	11
N Midlands	13	12	7	9	13	12	12	11	8	11
S Midlands	4	6	14	10	5	5	7	8	12	8
Urban	21	18	14	16	20	20	19	18	15	18

TABLE 30
THE AFFILLIATIONS OF THE ST. LOUIS LEXICON WITH THE MAJOR DIALECT AREAS OF THE EASTERN UNITED STATES (%)

	independent variable									
						age of informants				
dialect area	socioeconomic class of informants			gender of informants						
	upper	middle	lower	male	female	< 20	20 to 40	40 to 60	> 60	ALL
Midlands	23	25	23	24	22	23	23	24	25	24
North	31	27	26	27	29	30	29	28	26	28
South	12	20	20	20	21	21	21	20	19	20
N Midlands	21	20	20	20	21	21	20	20	19	20
S Midlands	13	15	16	15	15	14	15	15	16	15

Precisely why these patterns occur as they do will be addressed below as the answer to the third question posed in Chapter 1.

3. Why is the language of St. Louis is as it is?[2]

Thus far we have seen that although Gateway City speakers use linguistic forms typically associated with all five major dialect areas in the United States, Northern and North Midlands forms tend to be either preferred or perceived as "more correct" by the vast majority of speakers. Traditional dialectology would undoubtedly explain these preferences and perceptions as functions of immigration and settlement patterns, noting that Northern and North Midland states such as New York and Pennsylvania contributed large numbers of residents to the city during the second half of the nineteenth century, and that sizable ethnic populations of Germans and Irish (both of which exhibit some northernisms in their speech) also migrated to the area at that time. (For a brief, convincingly written essay outlining this kind of argument--with special attention to how "the Yankee served as a cultural and linguistic model for the German"--see Frazer 1979.) But this explanation ignores the equally large number of antebellum settlers from the South Midland States, the post-1900 influx of settlers from the Deep South, and the thousands of members of ethnic populations who brought no northernisms to the area. To rely on this kind of traditional dialectological explanation, then, raises as many questions as are putatively answered. Similarly, a sociolinguistic explanation that claims higher "standards of correctness" for urban St. Louis than the surrounding non-urban area (cf. Labov 1972: 299-300) does not address the problem of precisely why St. Louisans should perceive certain linguistic forms as more correct than others. In short, both the dialectological and sociolinguistic explanations are sound and logical as far as they go, but I would like to argue here that neither goes far enough--that, indeed, neither is sufficient to completely explain the prevalent language attitudes in St. Louis. I have collected data from subjective reaction tests--tests designed to elicit listeners' responses to various social levels of speech and the many speech variants associated with them (cf. Labov 1966, Labov 1972, Agheyisi and Fishman 1970, Lambert et al 1960, and Nader 1968)--that suggest a combined social and psychological approach is necessary for understanding Gateway City usage patterns. More specifically, I can show conclusively that the linguistic choices of St. Louisans are heavily influenced by their collective perceptions of what it means to be and sound like a "hoosier."

Before describing these subjective reaction tests and the data they produced, a brief digression is necessary to explain the term ***hoosier*** as as it is used and understood in St. Louis. Crinklaw (1976: 60) says it best:

> [St. Louisans] do not, as many think, use [hoosier] interchangably with hillbilly, which suggests a cute old fellow with a fishin' . . . pole, a jar of corn squeezin's and a corncob pipe. . . . [They] mean that displaced country man who moves into a city neighborhood and tears it up. As in, "First the hoosiers moved in, then the blacks." I guess you could say a hoosier is a hillbilly who's threatening.

Evidence for the widespread recognition of a definition of ***hoosier*** similar to Crinklaw's among St. Louisans can be found in Chapter 5, lexical item number 66 (PEJORATIVE TERM FOR A WHITE PERSON), to which one elderly middle–class female responded ***hillbilly*** and all 239 other informants responded ***hoosier***. Moreover, and what Crinklaw does not make explicit, is that few epithets in St. Louis carry the pejorative social connotations or the potential for eliciting negative responses that ***hoosier*** does. It may not be an overstatement to claim that Gateway City ***hoosier*** is the equivalent of a seriously spoken ***bastard*** or ***son of a bitch*** in other parts of the country (although those terms are of course also used in St. Louis). Nor is ***hoosier*** reserved only for undesirable members of society who move into the neighborhood and "tear it up," as Crinklaw says. If the driver of another car swerves in front of a St. Louisan who is also driving, the person who swerved is a hoosier. Similarly, if someone attends a social event or even merely appears in public and is inappropriately underdressed, that person is a hoosier. In short, any person whose behavior is perceived as nonstandard by a St. Louisan in any way can properly be termed a "hoosier."

To gather further evidence of the widespread use of ***hoosier*** as a term of pejoration in the Gateway City, I polled an additional 480 St. Louisans of various demographic backgrounds concerning their preferred terms of derogation for four demographically defined groups of people––members of the same race (black or white) and gender as the speaker, members of the same race but opposite gender, members of the opposite race but same gender, and members of the opposite race and opposite gender. The results of that poll can be found in Tables 31, 32, 33, and 34.

In Table 31, we see that of 120 white males surveyed, all cite ***hoosier*** as their first choice when referring to other white males. The same is true of white females, with one exception: one elderly middle–class woman prefers ***hillbilly***. Among blacks, the choices are more diverse. Although ***hoosier*** and ***nigger*** are the favorites among both males and females––***hoosier*** especially among those respondents who are over 40 and male or upper class and female, ***nigger*** especially among those respondents who are under 40 and male or middle or lower class and female––***spook*** and ***bitch*** each make progressively stronger showings as one descends through the male and female social classes, respectively. ***Coon*** and ***hillbilly*** also occur sporadically among both blacks and females.

Table 32 is similarly informative. Here we have 120 white females preferring ***hoosier*** exclusively when referring to white males, with 120 black females divided in usage between ***hoosier*** (preferred among those respondents over 40 years of age in each social class) and ***nigger*** (preferred among those respondents under 40 years of age in each social class). As for an equal number of males surveyed, those whites under 40 use both ***bitch*** and ***hoosier*** when referring to white females; white respondents over 40 much prefer ***hoosier***, however. Among black males, ***bitch***, ***hoosier***, and ***nigger*** all are popular when referring to black females: ***bitch*** is most popular with those respondents under 40 (and especially between 20 and 40), ***hoosier*** with those over 40, and nigger with those under 20.

Consider now Table 33. Of 120 males surveyed, most whites under the age of 40 in each social class refer to black males as ***niggers***; ***hoosier*** runs a close second, however, and is the favorite among most respondents over the age of 40. ***Coon***, ***hillbilly***, and ***spook*** occur sporadically and with no discernible pattern. Usage among black males is similarly divided: those over 40 prefer ***hoosier*** for white males, while those under 40 often use a different term––in this case ***hillbilly***. ***White trash*** also occurs sporadically and infrequently among blacks over 40. As for females, blacks prefer ***hoosier*** when referring to whites, with ***bitch*** enjoying some popularity among speakers under 40, ***white trash*** among speakers over 40, and ***hillbilly*** among a small number of speakers aged 40 to 60. Whites, on the other hand, largely prefer ***bitch*** if they are under 40, ***nigger*** if they are over 40, and use ***hoosier*** steadily at all age levels.

Finally, Table 34 depicts what St. Louisans call members of the opposite race and gender. Black females use ***hoosier*** exclusively to refer to white males; white females are divided between ***hoosier*** and ***nigger*** when referring to black males, the former used especially by respondents over the age of 20, the latter especially by those under 20. Among males, the patterns of usage are more diverse but no less interesting. The preferred term among all blacks is ***hoosier***, though ***bitch*** also occurs (especially in those under age 40), as does ***white trash*** (sporadically among those over 40, and with increasing frequency as one descends the social scale). For whites, ***nigger*** dominates among those under 40, ***hoosier*** among those over 40, ***bitch*** and *spook* occur consistently but weakly, and *coon* appears very infrequently among the eldest of the middle and lower classes.

Among the many conclusions to be drawn from these four tables, one especially begs to be noticed: with very few exceptions, *hoosier* is the preferred term of derogation among St. Louisans, and especially so when the object of derogation is white or, even more specifically, white and male.[3]

The subjective reaction tests that I used consisted of responses to sixty 30–second tape recordings––five males and five females from each race (black and white) representing speakers from each of the three major social divisions investigated––which were played in a random order for each of the 480 informants whose responses regarding preferred terms of derogation were given above in Tables 31–34. The recordings were typically answers to a query concerning childhood games, food items, or some other aspect of life in St. Louis, and the speakers were all people who, through preliminary interviews, had been eliminated from consideration for further use in the study. After listening to each of the tapes, the informants were asked to complete the following brief questionnaire:

(1) If you had to characterize this person in a word or two, what would the one or two words be, and would you consider that characterization positive or negative?

(2) If you had to guess, where would you say this person was probably born and raised, and would you consider that place positive or negative?

Answers to the first question were tabulated into three groups: those containing the word *hoosier*, all of which were marked "negative" and many of which contained a choice modifier or two (e.g., "some damn hoosier"); all other responses marked "negative"; and all responses marked "positive." Answers to the second question were also tabulated into three groups: those marked "negative" that specifically mentioned southern Mssouri or the Ozarks or both; all other negative responses; and all positive responses. The results of these subjective reaction tests are given in Table 35.

Several interesting patterns are revealed in Table 35. First, the vast majority of all St. Louisans have little or no trouble distinguishing upper– from lower–class speakers and display little or no hesitancy in labeling them as such. There is slightly more disagreement concerning attitudes toward the speech of the middle class––which is perhaps to be expected––but these people are much more often

TABLE 31
ST. LOUISANS' PREFERRED TERMS OF DEROGATION FOR PEOPLE OF THE SAME RACE AND GENDER AS THE SPEAKER

	demographic characteristics of respondents																							
	male																							
	white												black											
	upper class				middle class				lower class				upper class				middle class				lower class			
responses given	< 20	20 to 40	40 to 60	60 to 80	< 20	20 to 40	40 to 60	60 to 80	< 20	20 to 40	40 to 60	60 to 80	< 20	20 to 40	40 to 60	60 to 80	< 20	20 to 40	40 to 60	60 to 80	< 20	20 to 40	40 to 60	60 to 80
coon	0	0	0	0	0	0	0	0	0	0	0	0	0	0	1	2	0	1	0	1	0	0	2	1
hillbilly	0	0	0	0	0	0	0	0	0	0	0	0	0	1	0	0	0	0	1	1	0	0	1	0
hoosier	10	10	10	10	10	10	10	10	10	10	10	10	4	3	5	5	3	2	6	4	2	2	5	5
nigger	0	0	0	0	0	0	0	0	0	0	0	0	5	3	4	1	4	5	2	2	5	4	1	2
spook	0	0	0	0	0	0	0	0	0	0	0	0	1	3	0	2	3	2	0	2	3	4	1	2

TABLE 31 (cont.)

	demographic characteristics of respondents																							
	female																							
	white												black											
	upper class				middle class				lower class				upper class				middle class				lower class			
responses given	< 20	20 to 40	40 to 60	60 to 80	< 20	20 to 40	40 to 60	60 to 80	< 20	20 to 40	40 to 60	60 to 80	< 20	20 to 40	40 to 60	60 to 80	< 20	20 to 40	40 to 60	60 to 80	< 20	20 to 40	40 to 60	60 to 80
bitch	0	0	0	0	0	0	0	0	0	0	0	0	2	2	0	1	3	2	1	1	4	4	2	1
coon	0	0	0	0	0	0	0	0	0	0	0	0	0	0	1	0	0	1	0	0	0	0	2	1
hillbilly	0	0	0	0	0	0	0	1	0	0	0	0	0	0	1	0	0	0	0	1	0	1	0	1
hoosier	10	10	10	10	10	10	10	9	10	10	10	10	4	5	5	5	3	2	3	2	1	0	1	1
nigger	0	0	0	0	0	0	0	0	0	0	0	0	4	3	3	4	3	4	5	4	4	5	5	6
spook	0	0	0	0	0	0	0	0	0	0	0	0	0	0	0	0	1	1	1	0	1	0	0	0

TABLE 32
ST. LOUISANS' PREFERRED TERMS OF DEROGATION FOR PEOPLE OF THE SAME RACE BUT OPPOSITE GENDER AS THE SPEAKER

	demographic characteristics of respondents																							
	male																							
	white												black											
	upper class				middle class				lower class				upper class				middle class				lower class			
responses given	< 20	20 to 40	40 to 60	60 to 80	< 20	20 to 40	40 to 60	60 to 80	< 20	20 to 40	40 to 60	60 to 80	< 20	20 to 40	40 to 60	60 to 80	< 20	20 to 40	40 to 60	60 to 80	< 20	20 to 40	40 to 60	60 to 80
bitch	5	5	2	1	4	5	1	1	5	6	2	2	2	4	1	2	3	4	1	1	3	5	2	1
hoosier	5	5	8	9	6	5	9	9	5	4	8	8	2	3	6	5	3	2	7	8	2	3	7	7
nigger	0	0	0	0	0	0	0	0	0	0	0	0	6	3	3	3	4	4	2	1	5	2	1	2

TABLE 32 (cont.)

responses given	demographic characteristics of respondents: female, white, upper class, < 20	20 to 40	40 to 60	60 to 80	white, middle class, < 20	20 to 40	40 to 60	60 to 80	white, lower class, < 20	20 to 40	40 to 60	60 to 80	black, upper class, < 20	20 to 40	40 to 60	60 to 80	black, middle class, < 20	20 to 40	40 to 60	60 to 80	black, lower class, < 20	20 to 40	40 to 60	60 to 80
hoosier	10	10	10	10	10	10	10	10	10	10	10	10	4	4	8	8	4	5	7	9	3	4	8	8
nigger	0	0	0	0	0	0	0	0	0	0	0	0	6	6	2	2	6	5	3	1	7	6	2	2

TABLE 33
ST. LOUISANS' PREFERRED TERMS OF DEROGATION FOR SPEAKERS OF THE OPPOSITE RACE BUT SAME GENDER AS THE SPEAKER

	demographic characteristics of respondents																							
	male																							
	white												black											
	upper class				middle class				lower class				upper class				middle class				lower class			
responses given	< 20	20 to 40	40 to 60	60 to 80	< 20	20 to 40	40 to 60	60 to 80	< 20	20 to 40	40 to 60	60 to 80	< 20	20 to 40	40 to 60	60 to 80	< 20	20 to 40	40 to 60	60 to 80	< 20	20 to 40	40 to 60	60 to 80
coon	0	0	0	0	0	0	0	0	0	0	1	0	0	0	0	0	0	0	0	0	0	0	0	0
hillbilly	0	0	0	0	0	0	0	1	0	0	0	0	5	4	2	1	4	5	3	2	4	6	2	3
hoosier	2	3	5	5	3	2	6	5	1	3	6	7	5	6	6	9	6	5	6	5	6	4	6	5
nigger	8	7	5	5	7	8	3	4	9	6	2	2	0	0	0	0	0	0	0	0	0	0	0	0
spook	0	0	0	0	0	0	1	0	0	1	1	1	0	0	0	0	0	0	0	0	0	0	0	0
white trash	0	0	0	0	0	0	0	0	0	0	0	0	0	0	2	0	0	0	1	3	0	0	2	2

TABLE 33 (cont.)

responses given	demographic characteristics of respondents — female																							
	white												black											
	upper class				middle class				lower class				upper class				middle class				lower class			
	< 20	20 to 40	40 to 60	60 to 80	< 20	20 to 40	40 to 60	60 to 80	< 20	20 to 40	40 to 60	60 to 80	< 20	20 to 40	40 to 60	60 to 80	< 20	20 to 40	40 to 60	60 to 80	< 20	20 to 40	40 to 60	60 to 80
bitch	5	3	2	1	4	4	2	2	6	5	3	3	2	2	0	0	2	3	0	0	2	4	0	0
hillbilly	0	0	0	0	0	0	0	0	0	0	0	0	0	0	0	0	0	0	1	0	0	0	1	0
hoosier	2	4	3	4	3	4	4	5	1	2	3	3	8	8	9	8	8	7	9	7	8	6	7	8
nigger	3	3	5	5	3	2	4	3	3	3	4	4	0	0	0	0	0	0	0	0	0	0	0	0
white trash	0	0	0	0	0	0	0	0	0	0	0	0	0	0	1	2	0	0	0	3	0	0	2	2

TABLE 34
ST. LOUISANS' PREFERRED TERMS OF DEROGATION FOR PEOPLE OF THE OPPOSITE RACE AND GENDER OF THE SPEAKER

	demographic characteristics of respondents																							
	male																							
	white												black											
	upper class				middle class				lower class				upper class				middle class				lower class			
responses given	< 20	20 to 40	40 to 60	60 to 80	< 20	20 to 40	40 to 60	60 to 80	< 20	20 to 40	40 to 60	60 to 80	< 20	20 to 40	40 to 60	60 to 80	< 20	20 to 40	40 to 60	60 to 80	< 20	20 to 40	40 to 60	60 to 80
bitch	1	1	1	0	1	3	1	2	1	2	1	1	0	0	0	0	0	0	0	0	0	0	0	0
coon	0	0	0	0	0	0	0	1	0	0	0	1	0	0	0	0	0	0	0	0	0	0	0	0
hillbilly	0	0	0	0	0	0	0	0	0	0	0	0	0	0	0	0	0	0	1	1	0	0	0	0
hoosier	2	4	5	5	2	1	6	4	1	1	6	6	7	7	9	8	6	8	6	8	7	8	8	6
nigger	6	5	3	3	6	6	2	2	7	5	3	2	0	0	0	0	0	0	0	0	0	0	0	0
spook	1	0	1	2	1	0	1	1	1	2	0	0	0	0	0	0	0	0	0	0	0	0	0	0
white trash	0	0	0	0	0	0	0	0	0	0	0	0	0	0	0	1	0	0	2	1	0	0	2	3

TABLE 34 (cont.)

	demographic characteristics of respondents																							
	female																							
	white												black											
	upper class				middle class				lower class				upper class				middle class				lower class			
responses given	< 20	20 to 40	40 to 60	60 to 80	< 20	20 to 40	40 to 60	60 to 80	< 20	20 to 40	40 to 60	60 to 80	< 20	20 to 40	40 to 60	60 to 80	< 20	20 to 40	40 to 60	60 to 80	< 20	20 to 40	40 to 60	60 to 80
hoosier	5	6	7	7	4	5	7	8	5	7	6	7	10	10	10	10	10	10	10	10	10	10	10	10
nigger	5	4	3	3	6	5	3	2	5	3	4	3	0	0	0	0	0	0	0	0	0	0	0	0

TABLE 35
RESPONSES TO SUBJECTIVE REACTION TESTS*

white respondents and white speakers

	upper class																								
	male												female												
responses to	<20			20-40			40-60			60-80			<20			20-40			40-60			60-80			
question 1	Ho	Pe	Po	Ho	Pe	Po	Ho	Pe	Po	Ho	Pe	Po	Ho	Pe	Po	Ho	Pe	Po	Ho	Pe	Po	Ho	Pe	Po	
tapes 1-10 male:	0	0	10	0	0	10	0	0	10	0	0	10	0	0	10	0	0	10	0	0	10	0	0	10	
(upper class) female:	0	0	10	0	0	10	0	0	10	0	0	10	0	0	10	0	0	10	0	0	10	0	0	10	
tapes 11-20 male:	2	1	7	3	1	6	2	2	6	3	2	5	1	1	8	1	1	8	2	1	7	2	2	6	
(middle class) female:	1	1	8	1	0	9	1	2	7	2	1	7	0	1	9	1	1	8	1	0	9	2	1	7	
tapes 21-30 male:	6	3	1	7	1	2	7	2	1	9	1	0	5	4	1	6	3	1	6	4	0	8	1	1	
(lower class) female:	5	2	3	6	2	2	6	1	3	7	1	2	5	3	2	5	4	1	5	3	2	7	2	1	

responses to question 2		Oz	Pe	Po	Oz	Pe	Po	Oz	Pe	Po	Oz	Pe	Po	Oz	Pe	Po	Oz	Pe	Po	Oz	Pe	Po	Oz	Pe	Po
tapes 1-10	male:	0	0	10	0	0	10	0	0	10	0	0	10	0	0	10	0	0	10	0	0	10	0	0	10
(upper class)	female:	0	0	10	0	0	10	0	0	10	0	0	10	0	0	10	0	0	10	0	0	10	0	0	10
tapes 11-20	male:	1	2	7	2	2	6	3	1	6	3	2	5	1	1	8	1	1	8	1	2	7	2	2	6
(middle class)	female:	1	1	8	1	0	9	2	1	7	3	0	7	0	1	9	0	2	8	0	1	9	1	2	7
tapes 21-30	male:	5	4	1	4	4	2	4	5	1	5	5	0	6	3	1	4	5	1	7	3	0	6	3	1
(lower class)	female:	4	3	3	5	3	2	6	1	3	4	4	2	5	3	2	6	3	1	8	0	2	5	4	1

TABLE 35 (cont.)

white respondents and white speakers

		middle class																						
		male												female										
responses to		<20			20-40			40-60			60-80			<20			20-40			40-60			60-80		
question 1		Ho	Pe	Po	Ho	Pe	Po	Ho	Pe	Po	Ho	Pe	Po	Ho	Pe	Po	Ho	Pe	Po	Ho	Pe	Po	Ho	Pe	Po
tapes 1-10	male:	0	0	10	0	0	10	0	0	10	0	0	10	0	0	10	0	0	10	0	0	10	0	0	10
(upper class)	female:	0	0	10	0	0	10	0	0	10	0	0	10	0	0	10	0	0	10	0	0	10	0	0	10
tapes 11-20	male:	1	1	8	2	1	7	1	3	6	2	1	7	0	1	9	1	1	8	1	2	7	2	2	6
(middle class)	female:	1	0	9	1	1	8	2	1	7	1	1	8	1	1	8	1	0	9	0	1	9	1	1	8
tapes 21-30	male:	6	2	2	6	3	1	7	1	2	8	1	1	5	3	2	5	2	3	7	1	2	9	0	1
(lower class)	female:	5	3	2	6	2	2	6	1	3	7	2	1	6	1	3	5	3	2	6	2	2	8	1	1

responses to question 2		Oz	Pe	Po	Oz	Pe	Po	Oz	Pe	Po	Oz	Pe	Po	Oz	Pe	Po	Oz	Pe	Po	Oz	Pe	Po	Oz	Pe	Po
tapes 1-10	male:	0	0	10	0	0	10	0	0	10	0	0	10	0	0	10	0	0	10	0	0	10	0	0	10
(upper class)	female:	0	0	10	0	0	10	0	0	10	0	0	10	0	0	10	0	0	10	0	0	10	0	0	10
tapes 11-20	male:	1	1	8	1	2	7	2	2	6	2	1	7	0	1	9	1	1	8	2	1	7	1	3	6
(middle class)	female:	1	0	9	1	1	8	1	2	7	0	2	8	2	0	8	0	1	9	0	1	9	1	1	8
tapes 21-30	male:	5	3	2	4	5	1	4	4	2	6	3	1	4	4	2	5	2	3	6	2	2	7	2	1
(lower class)	female:	4	4	2	4	4	2	3	4	3	5	4	1	6	1	3	5	3	2	4	4	2	5	4	1

TABLE 35 (cont.)

white respondents and white speakers

responses to question 1		lower class																							
		male												female											
		<20			20-40			40-60			60-80			<20			20-40			40-60			60-80		
		Ho	Pe	Po	Ho	Pe	Po	Ho	Pe	Po	Ho	Pe	Po	Ho	Pe	Po	Ho	Pe	Po	Ho	Pe	Po	Ho	Pe	Po
tapes 1-10	male:	0	0	10	0	0	10	0	0	10	0	0	10	0	0	10	0	0	10	0	0	10	0	0	10
(upper class)	female:	0	0	10	0	0	10	0	0	10	0	0	10	0	0	10	0	0	10	0	0	10	0	0	10
tapes 11-20	male:	1	2	7	2	2	6	1	3	6	3	2	5	2	0	8	1	2	7	1	1	8	2	1	7
(middle class)	female:	1	1	8	1	2	7	2	2	6	1	2	7	3	1	6	2	0	8	1	0	9	1	1	8
tapes 21-30	male:	5	3	2	6	2	2	6	1	3	7	0	3	7	2	1	6	2	2	8	1	1	9	1	0
(lower class)	female:	6	2	2	6	1	3	7	1	2	6	3	1	7	2	1	6	2	2	7	1	2	8	1	1

responses to question 2		Oz	Pe	Po	Oz	Pe	Po	Oz	Pe	Po	Oz	Pe	Po	Oz	Pe	Po	Oz	Pe	Po	Oz	Pe	Po	Oz	Pe	Po
tapes 1-10	male:	0	0	10	0	0	10	0	0	10	0	0	10	0	0	10	0	0	10	0	0	10	0	0	10
(upper class)	female:	0	0	10	0	0	10	0	0	10	0	0	10	0	0	10	0	0	10	0	0	10	0	0	10
tapes 11-20	male:	0	3	7	2	0	8	2	2	6	3	2	5	2	0	8	1	2	7	1	1	8	1	2	7
(middle class)	female:	1	1	8	1	2	7	2	2	6	0	3	7	2	2	6	1	1	8	1	0	9	1	1	8
tapes 21-30	male:	4	4	2	3	5	2	5	2	3	4	3	3	6	3	1	6	2	2	5	4	1	7	3	0
(lower class)	female:	4	4	2	5	2	3	3	5	2	4	5	1	6	3	1	5	3	2	6	2	2	7	2	1

TABLE 35 (cont.)

white respondents and black speakers

upper class

responses to question 1		male <20			male 20-40			male 40-60			male 60-80			female <20			female 20-40			female 40-60			female 60-80		
		Ho	Pe	Po	Ho	Pe	Po	Ho	Pe	Po	Ho	Pe	Po	Ho	Pe	Po	Ho	Pe	Po	Ho	Pe	Po	Ho	Pe	Po
tapes 31-40	male:	0	0	10	0	0	10	0	0	10	0	0	10	0	0	10	0	0	10	0	0	10	0	0	10
(upper class)	female:	0	0	10	0	0	10	0	0	10	0	0	10	0	0	10	0	0	10	0	0	10	0	0	10
tapes 41-50	male:	1	2	7	0	3	7	2	2	6	0	2	8	0	3	7	1	2	7	1	1	8	1	2	7
(middle class)	female:	1	3	6	1	3	6	1	3	6	1	4	5	0	2	8	0	3	7	0	3	7	1	2	7
tapes 51-60	male:	4	5	1	4	5	1	5	3	2	3	4	3	4	4	2	4	4	2	5	5	0	5	5	0
(lower class)	female:	4	5	1	3	5	2	3	6	1	3	6	1	2	6	2	2	5	3	3	7	0	4	5	1

responses to question 2		Oz	Pe	Po	Oz	Pe	Po	Oz	Pe	Po	Oz	Pe	Po	Oz	Pe	Po	Oz	Pe	Po	Oz	Pe	Po	Oz	Pe	Po
tapes 31-40	male:	0	0	10	0	0	10	0	0	10	0	0	10	0	0	10	0	0	10	0	0	10	0	0	10
(upper class)	female:	0	0	10	0	0	10	0	0	10	0	0	10	0	0	10	0	0	10	0	0	10	0	0	10
tapes 41-50	male:	1	2	7	2	1	7	2	2	6	0	2	8	2	1	7	1	2	7	1	1	8	1	2	7
(middle class)	female:	2	2	6	1	3	6	3	1	6	2	3	5	1	1	8	1	2	7	1	1	8	1	2	7
tapes 51-60	male:	4	5	1	5	4	1	4	4	2	4	3	3	3	5	2	4	4	2	4	6	0	5	5	0
(lower class)	female:	5	4	1	4	4	2	4	5	1	5	4	1	3	5	2	6	1	3	4	6	0	6	3	1

TABLE 35 (cont.)

white respondents and black speakers

responses to question 1		middle class																							
		male												female											
		<20			20-40			40-60			60-80			<20			20-40			40-60			60-80		
		Ho	Pe	Po	Ho	Pe	Po	Ho	Pe	Po	Ho	Pe	Po	Ho	Pe	Po	Ho	Pe	Po	Ho	Pe	Po	Ho	Pe	Po
tapes 31-40	male:	0	0	10	0	0	10	0	0	10	0	0	10	0	0	10	0	0	10	0	0	10	0	0	10
(upper class)	female:	0	0	10	0	0	10	0	0	10	0	0	10	0	0	10	0	0	10	0	0	10	0	0	10
tapes 41-50	male:	0	3	7	0	3	7	1	2	7	1	4	5	0	3	7	0	3	7	2	2	6	1	3	6
(middle class)	female:	0	2	8	0	2	8	1	1	8	0	1	9	1	1	8	1	2	7	0	1	9	0	1	9
tapes 51-60	male:	5	2	3	5	3	2	6	2	2	7	2	1	4	3	3	6	3	1	6	3	1	6	2	2
(lower class)	female:	4	2	4	4	2	4	4	3	3	4	3	3	4	2	4	5	2	3	4	2	4	5	3	2

responses to question 2		Oz	Pe	Po	Oz	Pe	Po	Oz	Pe	Po	Oz	Pe	Po	Oz	Pe	Po	Oz	Pe	Po	Oz	Pe	Po	Oz	Pe	Po
tapes 31-40	male:	0	0	10	0	0	10	0	0	10	0	0	10	0	0	10	0	0	10	0	0	10	0	0	10
(upper class)	female:	0	0	10	0	0	10	0	0	10	0	0	10	0	0	10	0	0	10	0	0	10	0	0	10
tapes 41-50	male:	0	3	7	0	3	7	1	4	5	1	4	5	0	3	7	0	3	7	0	3	7	1	5	4
(middle class)	female:	0	1	9	0	1	9	0	0	10	0	1	9	1	2	7	1	3	6	1	2	7	1	3	6
tapes 51-60	male:	5	2	3	6	2	2	6	2	2	6	2	2	6	2	2	6	2	2	5	2	3	6	2	2
(lower class)	female:	4	2	4	4	1	5	5	1	4	3	0	7	4	1	5	4	2	4	3	1	6	5	2	3

TABLE 35 (cont.)

white respondents and black speakers

responses to question 1		lower class male <20 Ho	Pe	Po	20-40 Ho	Pe	Po	40-60 Ho	Pe	Po	60-80 Ho	Pe	Po	female <20 Ho	Pe	Po	20-40 Ho	Pe	Po	40-60 Ho	Pe	Po	60-80 Ho	Pe	Po
tapes 31-40	male:	0	0	10	0	0	10	0	0	10	0	0	10	0	0	10	0	0	10	0	0	10	0	0	10
(upper class)	female:	0	0	10	0	0	10	0	0	10	0	0	10	0	0	10	0	0	10	0	0	10	0	0	10
tapes 41-50	male:	1	2	7	1	2	7	2	1	7	1	1	8	2	2	6	1	2	7	0	1	9	2	1	7
(middle class)	female:	1	1	8	0	2	8	0	2	8	2	1	7	0	1	9	0	2	8	1	1	8	1	1	8
tapes 51-60	male:	5	2	3	5	2	3	6	3	1	6	2	2	4	1	5	5	1	4	5	2	3	5	2	3
(lower class)	female:	5	2	3	6	1	3	5	1	4	6	2	2	6	1	3	7	1	2	7	2	1	7	2	1

responses to question 2		Oz	Pe	Po	Oz	Pe	Po	Oz	Pe	Po	Oz	Pe	Po	Oz	Pe	Po	Oz	Pe	Po	Oz	Pe	Po	Oz	Pe	Po
tapes 31-40	male:	0	0	10	0	0	10	0	0	10	0	0	10	0	0	10	0	0	10	0	0	10	0	0	10
(upper class)	female:	0	0	10	0	0	10	0	0	10	0	0	10	0	0	10	0	0	10	0	0	10	0	0	10
tapes 41-50	male:	0	3	7	0	3	7	0	4	6	1	2	7	0	3	7	1	3	6	1	1	8	2	2	6
(middle class)	female:	1	2	7	1	2	7	1	1	8	2	2	6	0	3	7	0	1	9	2	1	7	1	2	7
tapes 51-60	male:	3	4	3	4	3	3	2	6	2	4	4	2	3	2	5	3	3	4	4	2	4	4	3	3
(lower class)	female:	4	3	3	4	3	3	4	3	3	5	2	3	3	4	3	4	4	2	4	4	2	4	3	3

TABLE 35 (cont.)

white respondents and black speakers

upper class

responses to question 1		male <20 Ho	Pe	Po	male 20-40 Ho	Pe	Po	male 40-60 Ho	Pe	Po	male 60-80 Ho	Pe	Po	female <20 Ho	Pe	Po	female 20-40 Ho	Pe	Po	female 40-60 Ho	Pe	Po	female 60-80 Ho	Pe	Po
tapes 31-40	male:	0	0	10	0	0	10	0	0	10	0	0	10	0	0	10	0	0	10	0	0	10	0	0	10
(upper class)	female:	0	0	10	0	0	10	0	0	10	0	0	10	0	0	10	0	0	10	0	0	10	0	0	10
tapes 41-50	male:	2	3	5	1	3	6	2	3	5	3	2	5	1	3	6	1	4	5	3	3	4	3	4	3
(middle class)	female:	1	3	6	1	2	7	2	2	6	2	2	6	2	2	6	1	2	7	1	3	6	2	3	5
tapes 51-60	male:	4	6	0	4	5	1	5	5	0	5	5	0	3	6	1	3	5	2	5	5	0	4	5	1
(lower class)	female:	3	5	2	3	5	2	4	6	0	5	5	0	4	5	1	4	5	1	5	4	1	5	5	0

responses to question 2		Oz	Pe	Po	Oz	Pe	Po	Oz	Pe	Po	Oz	Pe	Po	Oz	Pe	Po	Oz	Pe	Po	Oz	Pe	Po	Oz	Pe	Po
tapes 31-40	male:	0	0	10	0	0	10	0	0	10	0	0	10	0	0	10	0	0	10	0	0	10	0	0	10
(upper class)	female:	0	0	10	0	0	10	0	0	10	0	0	10	0	0	10	0	0	10	0	0	10	0	0	10
tapes 41-50	male:	1	4	5	0	4	6	2	3	5	2	3	5	1	3	6	1	4	5	2	4	4	2	5	3
(middle class)	female:	2	2	6	1	2	7	2	2	6	1	2	7	0	4	6	1	2	7	1	2	7	2	2	6
tapes 51-60	male:	2	7	1	3	6	1	3	6	1	3	7	0	2	7	1	2	6	2	3	7	0	5	5	0
(lower class)	female:	3	5	2	2	6	2	5	5	0	6	4	0	3	6	1	5	3	2	7	3	0	4	6	0

TABLE 35 (cont.)

white respondents and black speakers

responses to question 1		middle class																							
		male												female											
		<20			20-40			40-60			60-80			<20			20-40			40-60			60-80		
		Ho	Pe	Po	Ho	Pe	Po	Ho	Pe	Po	Ho	Pe	Po	Ho	Pe	Po	Ho	Pe	Po	Ho	Pe	Po	Ho	Pe	Po
tapes 31-40	male:	0	0	10	0	0	10	0	0	10	0	0	10	0	0	10	0	0	10	0	0	10	0	0	10
(upper class)	female:	0	0	10	0	0	10	0	0	10	0	0	10	0	0	10	0	0	10	0	0	10	0	0	10
tapes 41-50	male:	0	2	8	0	2	8	1	3	6	2	3	5	0	2	8	0	2	8	0	3	7	1	4	5
(middle class)	female:	0	2	8	0	2	8	1	2	7	1	2	7	1	1	8	0	3	7	0	3	7	1	2	7
tapes 51-60	male:	4	4	2	4	3	3	5	3	2	5	4	1	3	3	4	4	3	3	4	4	2	4	5	1
(lower class)	female:	3	4	3	3	4	3	3	3	4	3	4	3	2	3	5	2	3	5	3	4	3	2	5	3

responses to question 2		Oz	Pe	Po	Oz	Pe	Po	Oz	Pe	Po	Oz	Pe	Po	Oz	Pe	Po	Oz	Pe	Po	Oz	Pe	Po	Oz	Pe	Po
tapes 31-40	male:	0	0	10	0	0	10	0	0	10	0	0	10	0	0	10	0	0	10	0	0	10	0	0	10
(upper class)	female:	0	0	10	0	0	10	0	0	10	0	0	10	0	0	10	0	0	10	0	0	10	0	0	10
tapes 41-50	male:	0	3	7	1	2	7	1	2	7	2	3	5	0	3	7	0	3	7	2	2	6	2	2	6
(middle class)	female:	1	1	8	0	1	8	1	1	8	0	1	9	1	1	8	1	2	7	1	0	9	0	1	9
tapes 51-60	male:	4	3	3	4	4	2	5	3	2	4	5	1	3	4	3	4	5	1	3	6	1	4	4	2
(lower class)	female:	3	3	4	3	3	4	3	4	3	3	4	3	3	3	4	3	4	3	3	3	4	3	5	2

TABLE 35 (cont.)

white respondents and black speakers

		lower class																							
		male												female											
responses to		<20			20-40			40-60			60-80			<20			20-40			40-60			60-80		
question 1		Ho	Pe	Po	Ho	Pe	Po	Ho	Pe	Po	Ho	Pe	Po	Ho	Pe	Po	Ho	Pe	Po	Ho	Pe	Po	Ho	Pe	Po
tapes 31-40	male:	0	0	10	0	0	10	0	0	10	0	0	10	0	0	10	0	0	10	0	0	10	0	0	10
(upper class)	female:	0	0	10	0	0	10	0	0	10	0	0	10	0	0	10	0	0	10	0	0	10	0	0	10
tapes 41-50	male:	0	3	7	0	3	7	1	3	6	1	4	5	0	3	7	0	3	7	0	2	8	1	3	6
(middle class)	female:	0	2	8	0	3	7	0	2	8	1	3	6	1	3	6	1	3	6	0	4	6	1	3	6
tapes 51-60	male:	3	5	2	3	6	1	4	5	1	3	7	0	4	4	2	3	5	2	3	5	2	4	5	1
(lower class)	female:	3	4	3	2	5	3	2	6	2	2	7	1	3	5	2	2	6	2	2	5	3	3	5	2

responses to question 2		Oz	Pe	Po	Oz	Pe	Po	Oz	Pe	Po	Oz	Pe	Po	Oz	Pe	Po	Oz	Pe	Po	Oz	Pe	Po	Oz	Pe	Po
tapes 31-40	male:	0	0	10	0	0	10	0	0	10	0	0	10	0	0	10	0	0	10	0	0	10	0	0	10
(upper class)	female:	0	0	10	0	0	10	0	0	10	0	0	10	0	0	10	0	0	10	0	0	10	0	0	10
tapes 41-50	male:	2	1	7	1	2	7	2	2	6	2	1	7	1	2	7	2	2	6	1	1	8	2	2	6
(middle class)	female:	1	1	8	1	2	7	1	1	8	2	2	6	2	2	6	1	3	6	3	1	6	2	2	6
tapes 51-60	male:	3	5	2	4	5	1	5	4	1	4	5	1	3	5	2	3	5	2	5	3	2	4	4	2
(lower class)	female:	3	4	3	4	3	3	3	5	2	4	5	1	3	5	2	4	4	2	4	3	3	3	5	2

TABLE 35 (cont.)

black respondents and white speakers

upper class

responses to question 1		male <20 Ho	Pe	Po	20-40 Ho	Pe	Po	40-60 Ho	Pe	Po	60-80 Ho	Pe	Po	female <20 Ho	Pe	Po	20-40 Ho	Pe	Po	40-60 Ho	Pe	Po	60-80 Ho	Pe	Po
tapes 1-10	male:	0	0	10	0	0	10	0	0	10	0	0	10	0	0	10	0	0	10	0	0	10	0	0	10
(upper class)	female:	0	0	10	0	0	10	0	0	10	0	0	10	0	0	10	0	0	10	0	0	10	0	0	10
tapes 11-20	male:	3	1	6	3	2	5	3	2	5	4	2	4	2	1	7	3	1	6	2	2	6	3	3	4
(middle class)	female:	2	2	6	2	1	7	2	2	6	1	1	8	3	2	5	2	2	6	3	3	4	2	4	4
tapes 21-30	male:	4	5	1	4	5	1	4	5	1	5	5	0	5	2	3	4	4	2	4	4	2	5	4	1
(lower class)	female:	4	4	2	4	4	2	4	4	2	4	4	2	4	4	2	5	3	2	3	5	2	4	4	2

responses to question 2		Oz	Pe	Po	Oz	Pe	Po	Oz	Pe	Po	Oz	Pe	Po	Oz	Pe	Po	Oz	Pe	Po	Oz	Pe	Po	Oz	Pe	Po
tapes 1-10	male:	0	0	10	0	0	10	0	0	10	0	0	10	0	0	10	0	0	10	0	0	10	0	0	10
(upper class)	female:	0	0	10	0	0	10	0	0	10	0	0	10	0	0	10	0	0	10	0	0	10	0	0	10
tapes 11-20	male:	2	2	6	2	3	5	3	2	5	2	4	4	2	1	7	3	1	6	2	2	6	2	4	4
(middle class)	female:	3	1	6	1	2	7	3	1	6	2	0	8	0	5	5	3	1	6	4	2	4	2	4	4
tapes 21-30	male:	4	5	1	3	6	1	4	5	1	5	5	0	4	3	3	3	4	3	3	4	3	4	3	3
(lower class)	female:	4	4	2	4	4	2	4	4	2	3	5	2	5	3	2	2	6	2	6	2	2	2	6	2

TABLE 35 (cont.)

black respondents and white speakers

responses to question 1		middle class																							
		male												female											
		<20			20-40			40-60			60-80			<20			20-40			40-60			60-80		
		Ho	Pe	Po	Ho	Pe	Po	Ho	Pe	Po	Ho	Pe	Po	Ho	Pe	Po	Ho	Pe	Po	Ho	Pe	Po	Ho	Pe	Po
tapes 1-10	male:	0	0	10	0	0	10	0	0	10	0	0	10	0	0	10	0	0	10	0	0	10	0	0	10
(upper class)	female:	0	0	10	0	0	10	0	0	10	0	0	10	0	0	10	0	0	10	0	0	10	0	0	10
tapes 11-20	male:	2	2	6	2	2	6	3	2	5	4	2	4	2	2	6	3	2	5	2	2	6	3	2	5
(middle class)	female:	1	2	7	2	1	7	2	1	7	2	3	5	3	2	5	3	1	6	2	2	6	2	2	6
tapes 21-30	male:	5	2	3	5	2	3	4	2	4	4	3	3	5	3	2	5	2	3	4	5	1	5	4	1
(lower class)	female:	3	4	3	3	3	4	3	3	4	2	4	4	2	4	4	3	2	5	2	4	4	3	4	3

responses to question 2		Oz	Pe	Po	Oz	Pe	Po	Oz	Pe	Po	Oz	Pe	Po	Oz	Pe	Po	Oz	Pe	Po	Oz	Pe	Po	Oz	Pe	Po
tapes 1-10	male:	0	0	10	0	0	10	0	0	10	0	0	10	0	0	10	0	0	10	0	0	10	0	0	10
(upper class)	female:	0	0	10	0	0	10	0	0	10	0	0	10	0	0	10	0	0	10	0	0	10	0	0	10
tapes 11-20	male:	2	2	6	2	2	6	2	3	5	3	3	4	3	1	6	2	3	5	1	3	6	2	3	5
(middle class)	female:	1	2	7	2	1	7	1	2	7	1	4	5	3	2	5	2	2	6	2	2	6	2	2	6
tapes 21-30	male:	3	4	3	4	3	3	2	4	4	3	4	3	3	5	2	3	4	3	3	6	1	5	4	1
(lower class)	female:	2	5	3	3	3	4	2	4	4	3	3	4	3	3	4	3	2	5	2	4	4	2	5	3

TABLE 35 (cont.)

black respondents and white speakers

lower class

responses to question 1		male <20			20-40			40-60			60-80			female <20			20-40			40-60			60-80		
		Ho	Pe	Po	Ho	Pe	Po	Ho	Pe	Po	Ho	Pe	Po	Ho	Pe	Po	Ho	Pe	Po	Ho	Pe	Po	Ho	Pe	Po
tapes 1-10	male:	0	0	10	0	0	10	0	0	10	0	0	10	0	0	10	0	0	10	0	0	10	0	0	10
(upper class)	female:	0	0	10	0	0	10	0	0	10	0	0	10	0	0	10	0	0	10	0	0	10	0	0	10
tapes 11-20	male:	1	3	6	1	3	6	1	3	6	2	3	5	1	3	6	0	3	7	0	3	7	1	3	6
(middle class)	female:	0	3	7	0	2	8	0	2	8	1	4	5	1	2	7	1	2	7	0	3	7	1	4	5
tapes 21-30	male:	3	5	2	3	5	2	4	5	1	4	5	1	2	7	1	3	5	2	3	5	2	5	3	2
(lower class)	female:	2	5	3	2	5	3	2	6	2	2	6	2	1	7	2	1	7	2	2	7	1	2	6	2

responses to question 2		Oz	Pe	Po	Oz	Pe	Po	Oz	Pe	Po	Oz	Pe	Po	Oz	Pe	Po	Oz	Pe	Po	Oz	Pe	Po	Oz	Pe	Po
tapes 1-10	male:	0	0	10	0	0	10	0	0	10	0	0	10	0	0	10	0	0	10	0	0	10	0	0	10
(upper class)	female:	0	0	10	0	0	10	0	0	10	0	0	10	0	0	10	0	0	10	0	0	10	0	0	10
tapes 11-20	male:	1	2	7	2	1	7	2	2	6	2	2	6	1	2	7	1	1	8	0	3	7	1	1	8
(middle class)	female:	1	1	8	0	2	8	1	1	8	1	1	8	1	1	8	1	1	8	2	1	7	0	2	8
tapes 21-30	male:	4	4	2	4	5	1	4	5	1	5	5	0	3	5	2	2	7	1	3	6	1	4	5	1
(lower class)	female:	3	4	3	4	4	2	4	4	2	3	5	2	3	3	4	0	7	3	2	6	2	4	4	2

*The following abbreviations are used in reporting the responses to questions 1 and 2: Ho = *Hoosier*, perhaps with a modifier or two; Pe = all other pejorative labels (i.e., those judged negatively); Po = all positive labels or characteristics; Oz = the Ozarks or southern Missouri; Pe = all other pejorative locations (i.e., those judged negatively); Po = all places with positive labels.

them to be perceived negatively are characterized as "hoosiers": this is true of just over half of those members of the middle class who were judged negatively, and over three–fourths of the lower class. Curiously, male speakers tend to elicit the "hoosier" label more often than female speakers, though female judges are a bit freer in assigning the stigma than their male counterparts. Regarding the independent variable of age, there seems to be a positive correlation between increased age and willingness to call someone a hoosier; the correlation is especially strong for judges over the age of 60. Third, white speakers are perceived as hoosiers more frequently than are black speakers, and white judges seem more liberal in their use of the term than black judges. Finally, there is only slight disagreement among the various social classes concerning which speakers receive positive and negative labels and how often those labeled negatively are called "hoosiers." Apparently the lower–class judges, many of whom would undoubtedly also receive pejorative labels––"hoosier" among them––are either unaware of how they sound when they speak or willing to admit that they too use hoosier–sounding language.

The responses to the second question are equally revealing. Most telling, perhaps, is that over half of the respondents who judged a speaker negatively believed that person to have been born and raised in the Ozarks region of southern Missouri. There is clearly a correlation in the minds of these judges between the "nonstandard" linguistic habits of a "hoosier" and the stereotypical Ozarkian speaker. And we must note that it does not matter whether Ozarkian speakers *actually* have any speech traits in common with St. Louis hoosiers; what is salient here is that Gateway City residents *perceive* the two groups as sharing a similar if not identical language.

Why is the language of St. Louis as it is? Surely settlement and migration patterns and the city's status as an urban center helped to determine linguistic usage initially; perhaps these factors still play a role in St. Louisans' speech patterns today. But there is also an undeniable psycho–social component to language choice in St. Louis: speakers may often choose "Northern–sounding" forms because they wish to disociate with the Ozarkian South, the residents of which serve as the stereotypical hoosiers that call to mind such negative images in their city–dwelling counterparts.

Final Remarks

Linguistic variation in St. Louis, Missouri has proven to be an extremely fruitful topic for study: the phonology, morphology, syntax, and lexicon of the

Gateway City can now be clearly labeled primarily Northern and North Midland, though of course Southern and South Midland forms also persist because of the city's geographical location. Even more interesting, perhaps, are the reasons underlying this Northern and North Midland linguistic orientation; they include not only traditional explanations, but a more progressive one as well--one that is based on St. Louisans' collective perceptions of what it means to be and sound like a "hoosier" and where these hoosiers typically live. But however many questions this study has answered, it has also raised and left unanswered some new ones. What, for example, of the many linguistic forms that were found to vary in St. Louis but for which no other research exists? Does the way English is taught in the elementary and secondary schools reveal a bias for Northern and North Midland and against Southern and South Midland forms? (If so, how are teachers inculcated with these attitudes?) Will the linguistic patterns and attitudes of the Gateway City continue to persist relatively unchanged over the coming generations, or will the former be modified to accommodate new versions of the latter? These questions and others like them can serve as the focus of the next study on the language of St. Louis--a topic that will undoubtedly need to be returned to often if that language is ever to be described and explained completely.

NOTES

Chapter 1

[1] Faries's work was antedated by five master's theses, all of which were begun in 1953 at the University of Missouri (Columbia) under the direction of Professor George M. Pace and which, collectively, charted the lexicon of 37 of Missouri's 114 counties (see Shull 1953, Faries 1954, Hoskins 1954, Raithel 1954, and Sanders 1957). None, however, studied the lexicon of St. Louis or St. Louis County.

[2] Pace synopsizes his methods in the first two paragraphs of his article (p. 47):

> The statistics offered in this article derive from a tabulation of 148 idiolectal analyses. The tabulation was done by me, but the analyses are the work of students: specifically, students who over the past five years have taken under me a course in the structure of English. Chapter 9 of the textbook used [W. Nelson Francis, *The structure of American English*, 1958] contains a fourteen–page summary, by Raven I. McDavid, Jr., of the

> chief dialectal features of the Eastern United States. At the end of the course, the students were required to work through the summary, testing each feature in their speech but recording only those features which they were sure were present. The idiolectal analyses referred to above are their reports of their findings.
> The students are all native Americans, with no prolonged residence outside the state. Since they all are, or were, university students, they correspond (roughly) to the type–III informant of the Linguistic Atlas classification. As informants the students have certain obvious limitations. However, they have provided a large body of data on a subject about which little is known: general (i.e., non–Ozarkian) Missouri speech. As is usual with the work of students, cautious interpretation of the data is decidedly indicated. I present only the features which seem self–confirming because of the frequency with which they occur in the analyses.

He says further of his informants (p. 47, n. 3) that

> [They] are nearly all young adults (seniors majoring in English in order to teach in the secondary schools, graduate students and instructors in the University of Missouri English Department, a few high school teachers of English, and an occasional speech or foreign language major). Geographically the students represent the state reasonably well, except for the Ozarks. The students had been introduced to the summary early in the course and had transcribed the bulk of its phonetic items, in contrasting pronunciations, from my dictation. In an effort to discourage the manufacturing of statistics, the analyses were ungraded. The tabulation was done by hand, not by IBM cards.

And he concludes his article thus (p. 52):

> The evidence presented in this article applies, strictly speaking, only to the informants who furnished it: 148

> young, educated Missourians. Yet in my conclusion I shall risk generalizing, for there must surely be a relationship between their speech and that of numerous other Missouri natives. . . .

[3] The remarks of McDavid (1983: 4) are especially instructive:

> The amount of evidence gathered by a large-scale survey . . . is such that is is impossible for the investigator . . . to analyze all of the implications. . . . Consequently the directors of such surveys try to publish as much as possible of the full phonetic record. . . .

[4] One of the criticisms of Paddock (1981) was that he made "no attempt to compare Carbonear English with the English of any other area of North America" (Kinloch 1983: 187).

Chapter 2

[1]Bloomfield (1933: 497) has written that

> diffidence to one's speech is an almost universal trait. The observer who sets out to study a strange language or a local dialect, often gets data from his informants only to find them using entriely different forms when they speak among themselves. They count these latter forms inferior and are ashamed to give them to the observer. An observer may record a language entirely unrelated to the one he is looking for.

And the style–shifting studied by Labov and many others bears further witness to the phenomenon I witnessed.

[2] I have written elsewhere concerning the morality of collecting speech data surreptitiously (see Murray 1983a and Murray 1984e), and will not broach this very delicate subject again here.

[3] Labov (1972: 314, 320) has termed such linguistic variables "markers" to indicate that they vary both stylistically and socially. Markers may or may not "lie below the level of conscious awareness, [but] they will produce regular responses on subjective reaction tests" (1972: 314). If such markers eventually come to be "prominently labeled by society," they have become "stereotypes" (1972: 314). In the St. Louis area, at least, many of the sounds that my informants were wary of producing already seem to have reached the level of stereotypes, though they are probably not perceived nationally as such.

[4] Although I recorded only in public establishments, I always secured permission from the owners or managers in charge if I was going to spend an extended amount of time in the contexts collecting data.

[5] Most of what follows is a necessarily abbreviated sketch of the settlement history of St. Louis. A much fuller discussion appears in Johnson (1976: 12–30). A list of good resources for the study of Missouri's settlement history––which in many ways parallels that of the Gateway City––can be found in Faries (1967: 19–54). And see also the pertinent references listed in Johnson (1976: 101–03).

[6] Regarding the influx of Germans and Irish, Johnson (1976: 14) notes that between 1848 and 1852, nearly 30,000 Germans and 10,000 Irish raised the population of St. Louis from approximately 56,000 to over 96,000––an increase of over 40 percent.

[7] Each informant was coded SL1–SL240 to offer the possibility of checking to see whether the data were consistently being skewed by any of them (e.g., as when one or two would consistently give Southern responses to questions to which the rest

would offer a Northern response). Though no such skewing occurred, I had still originally hoped to publish the data informant by informant rather than demographic cell by demographic cell; but the informants became too numerous and the data too cumbersome to afford that luxury.

Chapter 3

[1]Some of the data reported here were originally presented in Murray (1983b) or Murray (1985c).

[2] The high front lax vowel does occur frequently among speakers of the Black English Vernacular, none of whom, as reported earlier in Chapter 2, served as informants in the present study.

[3] Traditional and popular explanations (mostly by non–St. Louisans) for what is perceived to be an aberrant pronunciation have been less than flattering (as is perhaps to be expected), and quazi–serious attempts to discover the nature of the "problem" appear at least annually in the feature column of some St. Louis journalist. The obvious linguistic explanation, of course, is that *sundae* has fallen prey to the phonological rule reducing unstressed vowels to centralized schwa. As to why only St. Louisans should apply that rule to *sundae*––if indeed they are the only ones to do so––I have no real explanation. According to Professor Donald Lance (personal communication, 4 November 1983 and 11 February 1984), Gateway City folklore dictates that turn– of–the–century soda jerks in a particular South St. Louis drug store invented the pronunciation because they received moral objections to the selling of ice cream sundaes (pronounced with [e] in the final syllable)––which were typically made with Coca– Cola, one of the secret ingredients of which was a derivative of cocaine––on Sundays (also pronounced with [e] in the final syllable). Apparently the mere thought of creating and vending–– on the Christian sabbath––drug–containing concoctions that were homophonous with the holy day of worship was sacrilegious. And rather than cease selling one day a week, which no doubt would have had a profound effect on sales

receipts, the merchants of one drug store eased their assailants' objections through the promotion of identically–made but non–homophonous ***sundaes*** (with schwa in the final syllable). A second, perhaps related reason is offered by Mr. Anthony J. Celebrezze, Jr., Attorney General for the State of Ohio (personal communication, 5 October 1985):

> . . . Sunday sales of soda water, lemonade, and pastries were banned in early Ohio. Most of the nation banned the sale of ice cream on Sunday because it was considered frivolous and a luxury. To make Sunday ice cream sales more acceptable, merchants began to top it with a scoop of fruit, marketing the new dish as healthy and nutritious. The new treat became very popular and is known today as an "ice cream sundae."

It is quite possible that the St. Louis pronunciation was then invented to further lessen any tension and make the new commodity even "more acceptable."

Chapter 6

[1]Of the more than 250 aspects of the language that I investigated, only 72, or almost 30%, could be listed in Table 23. Though a relatively small fraction of the total, the figure of 72 is by no means "small" on any absolute scale; thus while I would like to base the following discussion on considerably more substantial evidence, I do not believe the data in Table 23 are so few as to preclude the drawing of any significant conclusions.

[2] The data and conclusions given in this section were originally presented in Murray (1985d) and Murray (1985e).

[3] The reader should also see lexical item number 68 (PEJORATIVE TERM FOR A BLACK PERSON), in which half the informants reported using ***hoosier***. These

responses (which coincide with my own intuition as a native St. Louisan) throw into question that part of Crinklaw's definition that precludes *hoosier* from being applied to a black person.

[4] I have not addressed the questions of why the epithet *hoosier* exists or why it is widely used in St. Louis largely because they are at best of only tangential relevance to my central purpose here; however, the questions do have interesting answers (however speculative they may be), and perhaps it would not be inappropriate to consider them in this note. The actual linguistic origins of the word, as Baker and Carmony (1975: 72) point out, are shrouded in mystery:

> The origin of Hoosier has been much disputed, and a number of legends, anecdotes, and theories have arisen to explain the nickname. According to the most widely held account, pioneers in Indiana greeted visitors at the doors of their log cabins by calling out, "who's 'ere?" Another anecdote holds that a Louisville contractor named Samuel Hoosier preferred hiring Indiana men, and his employees were known as "hoosier men" or "Hoosiers." Other sources maintain that there was a lot of fighting in early Indiana taverns, and the frontiersmen scratched, gouged, and bit--often biting off noses and ears. Frequently following a fight a settler found an ear on the sawdust floor of a tavern and asked, "Whose ear?"
>
> Two other accounts agree that early settlers or Ohio River boatmen were vicious fighters and were called "hussars" because they fought like those European soldiers or "hushers" because they could hush any opponent. Other theories hold the term comes from the French houssieres, "the bushy places," or from an English dialectal word, "hoose," for roundworms. Apparently this disease of cattle caused the animals' hair to turn back and gave their eyes a wild look, as Indiana frontiersmen in their coonskin caps appeared to others. Still other explanations are that the nickname comes from hooza, an alleged Indian word for maize, from "huzza," an exclamation of early settlers, or from "hoozer," a southern dialectal word meaning something especially large.

Although Baker and Carmony are here speaking of the nickname of the state of Indiana, it is certainly no accident that that ***Hoosier*** and derogatory St. Louis ***hoosier*** should be phonologically and orthographically identical, so their comments can be extended to the latter as well. For the record, it may be worth noting that *Webster's Ninth Collegiate Dictionary* lists only the last– named of Baker and Carmony's suggestions as a possibility, and cites 1826 as the date of first recorded occurrence.

More certain is the geographic origin of the term. Baker and Carmony (1975: 72) again provide a useful point of departure:

> Field records for the Linguistic Atlas of the Middle and South Atlantic States . . . reveal that in the southern states Hooosier is a derogatory epithet connoting uncouthness and is synonomous with hick, hayseed, and hillbilly. Probably the term first was applied to early settlers in southern Indiana, themselves from southern states, who were considered uncouth rustics by their cousins back home in more established states.

Not coincidentally, the southern states were well– represented in St. Louis by heavy migrations after about 1900. It takes no stretch of the imagination to conclude that these settlers brought ***hoosier*** to the Gateway City with them, where it has remained largely intact as a term of derogation ever since. (***Hoosier*** also occurs in the argot of circus workers and pickpockets––in each case with negative connotations––but these specialty languages almost certainly acquired it from the South rather than the other way around.) As for the question of how exactly ***hoosier*** came to have such negative connotations, we can at best only speculate. The suggestion offered by Baker and Carmony (cited above) is one; another is that the term originally had only positive connotations––as the nickname of residents of Indiana––and then, when some of those residents migrated to the South and West after the Civil War, ***hoosier*** with negative connotations arose because of lingering differences of attitude concerning the question of slavery (Indiana was a Free State, and the entire South, of course––including Missouri––consisted of only Slave States). But as I said earlier, all of this is mere conjecture; I have found no hard evidence for the origins of pejorative ***hoosier***.

As to the future of ***hoosier*** in St. Louis, we can only speculate. Because the data in Tables 31 through 34 suggest that the term is sometimes more common among people over the age of 40 than under, a logical conclusion is that the epithet is waning and will eventually die an ignoble death at the hands of Father Time. Certainly terms such as ***bitch*** and ***nigger*** are alive and well and growing in popularity among younger Gateway City speakers; no doubt succeeding generations will find attractive and adopt entirely new derogatory language. In the meantime. however, ***hoosier*** remains alive and well in St. Louis, occupying as it does the honored position of being the city's number one term of derogation.

REFERENCES

Agheyisi, R., and J. A. Fishman. 1970. "Language Attitude Studies: A Brief Survey of Methodological Approaches." *Anthropological Linguistics* 12, 137–57.

Allison, Vernon C. 1929. "On the Ozark Pronunciation of 'It'." *American Speech* 4, 205–06.

Atwood, E. Bagby. 1953. *A Survey of Verb Forms in the Eastern United States.* Ann Arbor: Univ. of Michigan Press.

Bloomfield, Leonard. 1933. *Language.* New York: Holt, Rinehart, and Winston.

Carkeet, David. 1979. "The Dialects in *Huckleberry Finn.*" *American Literature* 51, 315– 32.

Carr, Joseph William, and Rupert Taylor. 1907. "A List of Words from Northwest Arkansas." *Dialect Notes,* Vol. III, part 3, 205–38.

Carriere, J.–M. 1939. "Creole Dialect of Missouri." *American Speech* 14, 109–19.

Crinklaw, Don. 1976. "Ladue Lockjaw, or How I Learned to Love the St. Louis Language." *St. Louisan* (October), 59–61.

Crumb, D. S. 1903. "The Dialect of Southeastern Missouri." *Dialect Notes*, Vol. II, part 5, 304–37.

Dakin, Robert F. 1971. "South Midland Speech in the Old Northwest." *Journal of English Linguistics* 5, 31–48.

Faries, Rachel B. 1954. "A Survey of the Vocabulary of Seven Northeast Central Missouri Counties." M.A. Thesis, Univ. of Missouri.

———————. 1967. "A Word Geography of Missouri." Ph.D. Dissertation, Univ. of Missouri.

Flexner, Stuart Berg. 1976. *I Hear America Talking.* New York: Simon and Schuster.

Frazer, Timothy C. 1973. "The Dialect Subareas of the Illinois Midland." Ph.D. Dissertation, Univ. of Chicago.

———————. 1978. "South Midland Pronunciation in the North Central States." *American Speech* 53, 40–48.

———————. 1979. "The Speech Island of the American Bottoms: A Problem in Social History." *American Speech* 54, 185– 93.

Hoskins, Jewel Mae. 1954. "A Survey of the Vocabulary of Seven Eastern Missouri Valley Counties." M.A. Thesis, Univ. of Missouri.

Johnson, Robert L. 1976. "A Brief Study of Dialect in St. Louis." M.A. Thesis, Univ. of Missouri.

Kinlock, A. M. 1983. Review of Harold Paddock, *A Dialect Survey of Carbonear, Newfoundland. Publications of the American Dialect Society*, No. 68 (University, Alabama: Univ. of Alabama Press).

Kurath, Hans. 1949. *A Word Geography of the Eastern United States.* Ann Arbor: Univ. of Michigan Press.

-----------, and Raven I. McDavid, Jr. 1961. *The Pronunciation of English in the Atlantic States.* Ann Arbor: Univ. of Michigan Press.

Labov, William. 1966. *The Social Stratification of English in New York City.* Washington, D.C.: Center for Applied Linguistics.

-----------. 1972. *Sociolinguistic Patterns.* Philadelphia: Univ. of Pennsylvania Press.

Laird, Charlton. 1970. *Language in America.* Englewood Cliffs: Prentice-Hall.

Lambert, Wallace E., et al. 1960. "Evaluational Reactions to Spoken Languages. *Journal of Abnormal and Social Psychology* 60, 44-57.

Lance, Donald M. 1974a. "Dialect Divisions in Missouri." Paper presented to the Midwestern Regional Meeting of the American Dialect Society, 1 November.

-----------. 1974b. "Missouri and Surrounding States." Paper presented to the Annual Meeting of the American Dialect Society, 27 December.

-----------. 1975. "Missouri Dialects Revisited." Paper presented to the Missouri Academy of Sciences, 26 April.

-----------. 1977. "Determining Dialect Boundaries in the United States by Means of Automatic Cartography." *Germanistiche Linguistik* 3-4, 289-303.

-----------, and Rachel B. Faries. 1985. "Dialect Divisions in Missouri." Paper presented to the Midwestern Regional Meeting of the American Dialect Society, 7 November.

Lance, Donald M., and Steven M. Slemons. 1976. "The Use of the Computer in Plotting the Geographical Distribution of Dialect Items." *Computers and the Humanities* 10, 221-29.

McDavid, Raven I., Jr. 1972. "The Principal Dialect Areas of the United States." In David L. Shores, ed., *Contemporary English: Change and Variation* (New York: Lippincott), 26-41. Rpt. from W. Nelson Francis, *The Structure of American*

English (New York: Ronald, 1958).

-----------. 1983. "Linguistic Geography." In *Needed Research in American English* (1984), pp. 4–28. *Publications of the American Dialect Society*, No. 71 (University, Alabama: Univ. of Alabama Press).

Malmstrom, Jean, and Annabel Ashley. 1963. *Dialects--U.S.A.* Champaign: NCTE.

Marckwardt, Albert H. 1957. "Principal and Subsidiary Dialect Areas in the North–Central States." *Publications of the American Dialect Society*, No. 27 (University, Alabama: Univ. of Alabama Press), pp. 3–15.

Murray, Thomas E. 1982. "Speaking with Style: Language Variation in Graduate Students. Ph.D. Dissertation, Indiana Univ.

-----------. 1983a. "Funeral Parlor Talk." Paper presented to the Joint Meeting of the Dictionary Society of North America and the American Dialect Society, 11 June. To appear in a collection of essays ed. W. Bruce Finnie.

-----------. 1983b. "Some Sounds of St. Louis: A Social and Stylistic Appraisal." Paper presented to the Midwestern Regional Meeting of the American Dialect Society, 3 November.

-----------. 1984a. "Folk Etymology in the Streets of St. Louis." Paper presented to the Midwestern Regional Meeting of the American Name Society, 3 November. To appear in *Names.*

-----------. 1984b. "Mortuarial Sociolinguistics: Observations on the Language Used in Funeral Homes." *Research Record* 1: 43–57.

-----------. 1984c. "*Poppy Show.*" *American Speech* 59: 99–122.

-----------. 1984d. "On the Primacy of Context in Stylistic Language Variation: A Theoretical Perspective." Paper presented in the Colloquium Series of the Department of Linguistics, The Ohio State University, 8 May.

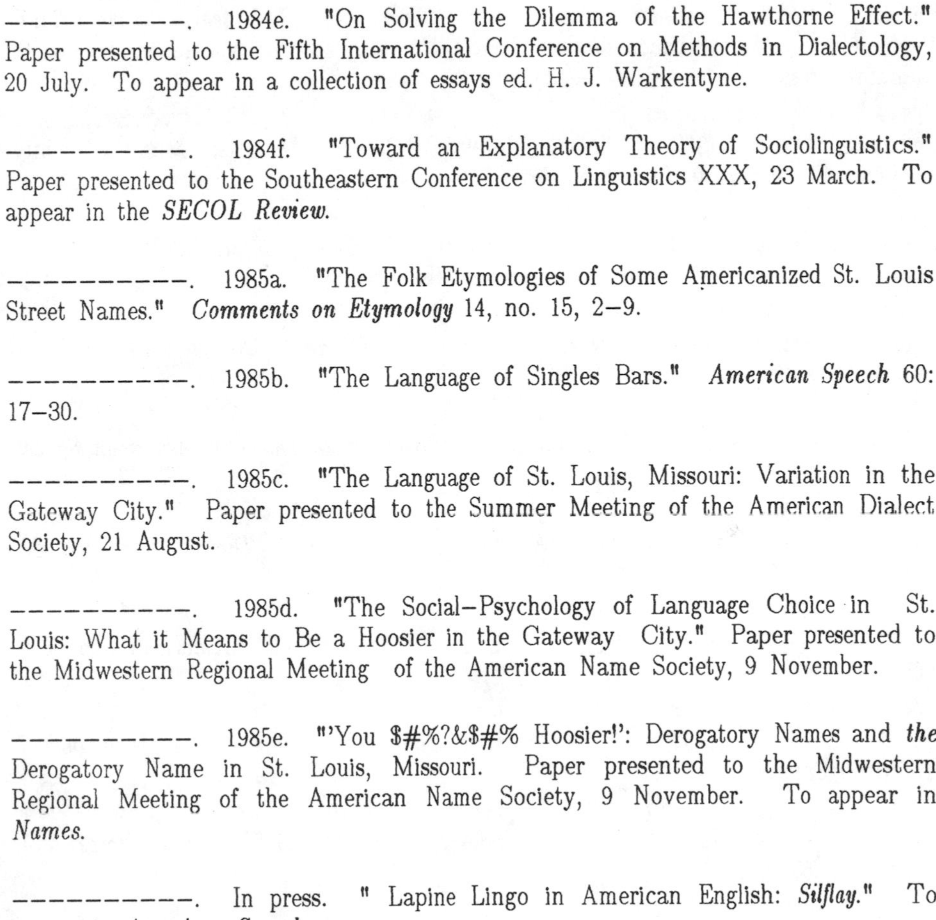

———————————. 1984e. "On Solving the Dilemma of the Hawthorne Effect." Paper presented to the Fifth International Conference on Methods in Dialectology, 20 July. To appear in a collection of essays ed. H. J. Warkentyne.

———————————. 1984f. "Toward an Explanatory Theory of Sociolinguistics." Paper presented to the Southeastern Conference on Linguistics XXX, 23 March. To appear in the *SECOL Review.*

———————————. 1985a. "The Folk Etymologies of Some Americanized St. Louis Street Names." *Comments on Etymology* 14, no. 15, 2–9.

———————————. 1985b. "The Language of Singles Bars." *American Speech* 60: 17–30.

———————————. 1985c. "The Language of St. Louis, Missouri: Variation in the Gateway City." Paper presented to the Summer Meeting of the American Dialect Society, 21 August.

———————————. 1985d. "The Social–Psychology of Language Choice in St. Louis: What it Means to Be a Hoosier in the Gateway City." Paper presented to the Midwestern Regional Meeting of the American Name Society, 9 November.

———————————. 1985e. "'You $#%?&$#% Hoosier!': Derogatory Names and *the* Derogatory Name in St. Louis, Missouri. Paper presented to the Midwestern Regional Meeting of the American Name Society, 9 November. To appear in *Names.*

———————————. In press. " Lapine Lingo in American English: *Silflay.*" To appear in *American Speech.*

Nader, Laura. 1968. "A Note on Attitudes and the Use of Language." In J. A. Fishman, ed., *Readings in the Sociology of Language* (The Hague: Mouton), pp. 276–81.

Pace, George B. 1965. "On the Eastern Affiliations of Missouri Speech." *American Speech* 40: 47–52.

Paddock, Harold. 1981. *A Dialect Survey of Carbonear, Newfoundland. Publications of the American Dialect Society,* No. 68. University, Alabama: Univ. of Alabama Press.

Pederson, Lee. 1967. "Mark Twain's Missouri Dialects: Marion County Phonemics." *American Speech* 42, 261–78.

Raithel, Erna E. 1954. "A Survey of the Vocabulary of Eight West Central Missouri Counties." M.A. Thesis, Univ. of Missouri.

Randolph, Vance. 1926. "Word–List from the Ozarks." *Dialect Notes,* Vol. V, part 9, 396–405.

———————. 1927a. "The Grammar of the Ozark Dialect." *American Speech* 3: 1–11.

———————. 1927b. "More Words from the Ozarks." *Dialect Notes,* Vol. V, part 10, 472–79.

———————. 1927c. "The Ozark Dialect in Fiction." *American Speech* 2: 283–89.

———————. 1928a. "A Possible Source of Some Ozark Neologisms." *American Speech* 4: 116–17.

———————. 1928b. "Verbal Modesty in the Ozarks." *Dialect Notes,* Vol. VI, part 1, 57–64.

———————. 1929a. "Is There an Ozark Dialect?" *American Speech* 4: 203–04.

———————. 1929b. "A Third Ozark Word–List." *American Speech* 5: 16–21.

———————. 1931. "Recent Fiction and the Ozark Dialect." *American Speech* 8: 47–53.

———————————. 1933. "A Fourth Ozark Word–List." *American Speech* 8: 47–53.

———————————, and Nancy Clemens. 1936. "A Fifth Ozark Word–List." *American Speech* 11, 314–18.

Randolph, Vance, and Anna A. Ingleman. 1928. "Pronunciation in the Ozark Dialect." *American Speech* 3: 401–07.

Randolph, Vance, and Patti Sankee. 1930a. "Dialect Survivals in the Ozarks, I." *American Speech* 5: 198–208.

———————————. 1930b. "Dialect Survivals in the Ozarks, II." *American Speech* 5: 264–69.

———————————. 1930c. "Dialectal Survivals in the Ozarks, III." *American Speech* 5: 424–30.

Randolph, Vance, and Isabel Spradley. 1933. "Quilt Names in the Ozarks." *American Speech* 8: 33–36.

Randolph, Vance, and George P. Wilson. 1953. *Down in the Holler: A Gallery of Ozark Folk Speech.* Normal: Univ. of Oklahoma Press.

Roethlisberger, F. J. 1949. *Management and Morale.* Cambridge: Harvard Univ. Press.

Sanders, Gordon Ray. 1957. "A Survey of the Vocabulary of Seven Northeast Missouri Valley Counties." M.A. Thesis, Univ. of Missouri.

Shull, Bettie Bronson. 1953. "A Survey of the Vocabulary of Seven Northeast Missouri Counties." M.A. Thesis, Univ. of Missouri.

Shuy, Roger W. 1967. *Discovering American Dialects.* Champaign: NCTE.

Taylor, Jay L. B. 1923. "Snake County Talk." *Dialect Notes*, Vol. V, part 6, 197–225.

Trudgill, Peter. 1974a. *The Social Differentiation of English in Norwich.* Cambridge: Cambridge Univ. Press.

———————————. 1974b. *Sociolinguistics: An Introduction.* New York: Penguin.

Underwood, Gary N. 1981. *The Dialect of the Mesabi Range. Publications of the American Dialect Society,* No. 67. University, Alabama: Univ. of Alabama Press.

Weeks, R. L. 1891. "Notes from Missouri." *Dialect Notes,* Vol. I, part 5, 235–42.

Wolfram, Walt. 1969. *A Sociolinguistic Description of Detroit Negro Speech.* Washington, D.C.: Center for Applied Linguistics.

———————————, and Roger W. Shuy. 1974. *The Study of Social Dialects in American English.* Englewood–Cliffs: Prentice–Hall.